Deep Mysteries

Deep Mysteries

God, Christ, and Ourselves

Aidan Nichols, OP

LEXINGTON BOOKS/FORTRESS ACADEMIC
Lanham • Boulder • New York • London

Published by Lexington Books/Fortress Academic
Lexington Books is an imprint of The Rowman & Littlefield Publishing Group, Inc.
4501 Forbes Boulevard, Suite 200, Lanham, Maryland 20706
www.rowman.com

Unit A, Whitacre Mews, 26-34 Stannary Street, London SE11 4AB

British Library Cataloguing in Publication Information Available

Library of Congress Cataloging-in-Publication Data

Names: Nichols, Aidan, author.
Title: Deep mysteries : God, Christ and ourselves / Aidan Nichols OP.
Description: Lanham : Fortress Academic, 2018. | Includes bibliographical references and index.
Identifiers: LCCN 2018040571 (print) | LCCN 2018052902 (ebook) | ISBN 9781978704848 (elec-
    tronic) | ISBN 9781978704831 (cloth : alk. paper)
Subjects: LCSH: Jesus Christ--Historicity. | Jesus Christ--Biography. | Mystery. | Spirituality--Chris-
    tianity.
Classification: LCC BT303.2 (ebook) | LCC BT303.2 .N47 2018 (print) | DDC 232--dc23
LC record available at https://lccn.loc.gov/2018040571

Printed in the United States of America

Contents

Preface

This book is a cocktail of ingredients that are not usually combined. Its account of the New Testament is largely derived from Evangelical Protestant sources, mixed in with some older Roman Catholic exegesis. This is because I wish to maintain the full historicity of the principal Gospel events whose significance lies at the heart of this work. My reflection on those events is guided by the Fathers of the Church and the historic Liturgies. (Among the former, I am especially indebted to St. Leo, whose approach I find congenial.) It extends to the most inspirational of modern theologians who, for me, are Hans Urs von Balthasar in the Catholic sphere and Sergius Bulgakov in the Orthodox (the latter, however, will appear here only in a comparatively minor supporting role).

The way in which I relate the New Testament events to the spiritual deployment of those events in the life of the believing and worshipping Church is taken essentially from St. Thomas Aquinas. I follow the main lines of his account of the "causality" of the chief mysteries of the life of Christ. And incidentally, the potency of those mysteries has not been lost on artists—so I also make appeal to the way they are refracted in visual art, especially the art of the icon.

Finally, my basic idea in writing this book derives from the early twentieth century Irish Benedictine monk, Dom Columba Marmion, beatified by Pope John Paul II. Marmion's *Christ in His Mysteries* was the first work of solid spiritual theology I ever read, while working as a volunteer in the Legion of Mary hostel for the destitute in Dublin 7, during a gap year between leaving school and going to university. I had behind me years of Anglican worship. As a Roman Catholic, I had recently been instructed, as was usual then in England, by the "Penny Catechism." But Marmion opened my eyes to riches untold.

Blackfriars, Cambridge
Pentecost, 2018

Chapter One

The Witnesses

How credible are the New Testament reports about the main events in the life of Christ and the origins of his Church? Two initial objections, which we can call historical in character, are likely to arise. The first concerns the written records of that testimony, the New Testament texts—above all the Gospels—have they been handed down in their integrity? Or were they perhaps tampered with in transmission, notably in the early centuries of the Common Era? Graham Stanton, an exegete working in the secular academy, remarks in his report on state-of-the-art scholarship in this area:

> In recent decades important steps forward have been taken. The discovery of papyri which pre-date the great fourth-century uncial manuscripts has been a major advance. Even though the second and third century papyri are often fragmentary, they confirm the general reliability of the great fourth-century uncials which contain the full text of the Gospels. [1]

Then in the second place, there is a question about the origins, composition, and dating of the texts—above all, once again, of the Gospels. Concerning the handing on of memories about Jesus, is a general skepticism warranted? With pardonable irritation, the mid-twentieth century exegete Vincent Taylor, pointed out that Jesus's first disciples were hardly

> translated to heaven immediately after the Resurrection. . . . The hundred and twenty at Pentecost did not go into permanent retreat; for at least a generation they moved among the young, Palestinian communities, and through preaching and fellowship their recollections were at the disposal of those who sought information. [2]

Without further ado, let us introduce the principal witnesses among those apostles and "apostolic men."

Among them, I take first Saint Paul. Paul's early letters were collected together and "published" in codex form—which is possibly the origin of the Christian preference for the codex over against the much more widespread "roll."[3] That preference is especially notable where Christian reproduction of sacred texts, and above all the Gospels, was concerned. Yet considered as informational sources for the life of Jesus, the Pauline letters, the earliest of them written less than twenty years after the Crucifixion, may seem at first sight stony ground.

Paul does not cite any Gospel books—which conceivably, toward the end of his life he might have done. It is arguable that both Matthew's Gospel book and Luke's were produced before the apostle's letter-writing activity ceased, around the end of the 50s of the first century of our era.[4] Nor does Paul give much information about Jesus's life (and teaching) from the oral tradition, the earliest "apostolic preaching," which preceded the making of all such books.

By itself, reticence in citing written sources might not be odd. While the original apostles still lived and could be heard *viva voce*, it was less important to refer to their writings. Moreover, Christians had no equivalent to the synagogue schools where those writings could be taught and studied. Nor did they have, as yet, a procedure for officially recognizing certain texts as especially authoritative. And in any case, the expense of parchment, and its consequent rarity, would discourage appeal to books.[5] Yet the Gospel books themselves draw on the all-important common oral tradition of the sayings and doings of Jesus. So in this perspective, Paul's extreme simplification of data about the life of Jesus is surprising, and, more than surprising, it is striking.

That does not make Paul's letters a *tabula rasa* for the question of the Jesus of history. Fragments of catechesis, precise and circumstantial in kind, touching the Last Supper and the Resurrection, can be found in his Corinthian correspondence. Among moral prescriptions, Paul can distinguish, as in First Corinthians (7:10), directives that issue from Jesus himself, carefully separating these from his own more personal advice. In the Letters to Rome and Corinth, Paul's counsels reflect evangelical sayings (for instance, Romans 12:11–14; I Corinthians 4:12–13, 9:14, 12:3),[6] or recall virtues Jesus showed, such as gentleness and modesty (II Corinthians 10:1), a predilection for the poor and an effective practice of poverty (II Corinthians 8:9), as well as charity toward enemies (Romans 12:19–21).[7] A basic biography of Jesus could be gleaned from references scattered about the Letters.

A summary of the biographical information about Jesus that can be pieced together from the Pauline epistles would include his descent from Abraham and David (Galatians 3:16, Romans 1:3), his upbringing in the Jewish law (Galatians 4:4), his gathering together disciples, including Cephas (Peter) and

John, and his having a brother named James (Galatians 1:19, 2:9), his impeccable character and exemplary life (e.g. Philippians 2:6–8; II Corinthians 8:9; Romans 15:3, 8), his Last Supper and betrayal (1 Corinthians 11:23–25), and numerous details surrounding his death and resurrection (e. g. Galatians 3:1; 1 Thessalonians 2:15; 1 Corinthians 15:4–8).[8]

Such allusions are the more impressive for not being concerted.[9] They show how much Paul had learned, information-wise, beyond his "Damascus Road" experience of the risen Christ in the year 33. That must mean, more specifically, what he learned from his visit to the Jerusalem apostles two years later and especially from their leading spokesman, St. Peter.[10]

There is something providential about this economy of data. A witness who, on the basis of direct historical contact, was more familiar with Jesus's life would probably have been less able to produce what a French scholar called an "impression of the ensemble, global, disengaged from the confused richness of concrete detail and the overlapping of too close perspectives."[11] Léonce de Grandmaison wrote,

> In the manner of great contemplatives who, for the sake of unification and deepening, deliberately let particular knowledge of divine things be impoverished in them, St. Paul seems sometimes to retain, of the human career of his Master, only the beginning and the end, the "coming in the flesh" and the "entry into glory" by the painful way of the Cross. It is on the Cross indeed that Jesus appears as the head of redeemed humanity. Without being for all that indifferent to the [time] in-between, the apostle lets it go, reducing to the essential data the basis of fact on which he builds. The prodigious abbreviation of the letter to the Philippians which leads us on a straight line from the incarnation to Calvary is not an exception in Paul's work. . . . The theological vision of the apostle has swallowed up in the life of the Word made flesh all that is not the indispensable foundation of the redemption.[12]

So speaks—with consummate elegance—a French Jesuit exegete of the early twentieth century. The English Evangelical scholar John Wenham, writing much more recently, makes the same point more prosaically, if also more succinctly. "The whole Jesus tradition was necessary to make the gospel claim intelligible, but in *paraenesis* [exhortation] all was secondary to its great climax."[13]

The "great climax" in question concerns the way that the One who descended was also the One who, through his Cross and Resurrection, ascended, so as to bring human beings with full effect into the divine realm. And here something must be said without further ado. St. Paul's language about Jesus is inexplicable unless he regarded this fellow Jew as, in some sense compatible with the monotheism of the Old Testament, One who was personally divine.

Paul regarded the resurrected Jesus as occupying a unique position of heavenly authority and honor, and he wrote of the exalted Christ and reverenced him in ways that seem to require us to conclude that Paul treated him as divine.[14]

And the American New Testament scholar Larry Hurtado, just cited, adds to this claim a reference to its—highly significant—unoriginality.

[N]othing in Paul's letters indicates any awareness that his fundamental view of Christ was unique or that he had made any serious innovation in the way Christians before him had regarded the exalted Jesus, however much he may have had his own emphases in the articulation of his message.[15]

So much for St. Paul. I come now to the synoptic evangelists, Matthew, Mark, and Luke. De Grandmaison had what sounds like a sensible approach to the "Synoptic Problem"—the thorny question of the literary inter-relation of the First, Second, and Third Gospels as found in the New Testament Canon.

The simplest solution consists in saying that Matthew, Mark and Luke have used, each in his own way, and independently of the others, oral sources, fixed and so to say stereotyped by traditional procedures.[16]

Yet fixed or stereotyped oral sources are no longer available for confirmatory inspection. That is part of the "Synoptic Problem"! There might be a simpler solution still. Could it be that the differences, sometimes very minor, between the Synoptic Gospels simply reflect the variety of occasions on which Jesus said almost—but not quite—the same thing? That cannot be ruled out.

[The sayings'] similarities derive from a common source in the mind of Jesus, rather than from a single utterance of his lips. It is inevitable that an itinerant preacher must repeat himself again and again, sometimes in identical words sometimes with slight variations, sometimes with new applications; sometimes an old idea will appear in an entirely new dress.[17]

The "Seventy," that substantial group of disciples who heard Jesus during the public ministry, may have included some major transmitters of words overheard. But the principal source will surely be the inner group of the "Twelve," with St. Peter at their head, during their lengthy period of common preaching in Jerusalem.

Why Jerusalem, to which city, after the Galilean Resurrection appearances those of the Twelve who witnessed the Risen Lord there, made haste to return? Larry Hurtado explains the profound significance of Jerusalem as a locale:

The Galilean followers of Jesus (e.g., Cephas, John and James Zebedee, James the brother of Jesus) took pains to form themselves as a group in *Jerusalem*, which can only mean that they saw themselves as witnesses to the nation and sought to position themselves in its ancestral capital and worship center. This is also fully compatible with their royal-messianic emphasis that was a feature of their interpretation of Jesus. They proclaimed Jesus as Israel's Messiah, the divinely appointed heir of David and the one through whom Israel could now hope to obtain forgiveness of her sins and redemption (e.g., Acts 2:36, 39, 4:18–21). It is therefore also perfectly understandable that the Jerusalem church made a special point of the temple as a place for giving their witness to Jesus. The place of the temple in the canonical Gospels preserves the notion from the early Judaean Christian circles that, as Messiah, Jesus has a rightful claim over it.[18]

True, Jesus had predicted the downfall of the Temple. But until that event came about it retained all its significance.

At their Jerusalem base, the Twelve had a threefold advantage. They were eyewitnesses; they had enjoyed a special intimacy with the Lord; and they were in possession of his mandate to preach and teach. They would not, of course, have been unique in the first respect. There were more eyewitnesses than just themselves. This undeniably true observation naturally extends the range of those whose voices should count. The British New Testament scholar Richard Bauckham sets out the evidence for the view that

> up to the writing of the Gospels, gospel traditions were connected with named and known eyewitnesses, people who had heard the teaching of Jesus from his lips and committed it to memory, people who had witnessed the events of his ministry, death and resurrection and themselves had formulated the stories about these events that they told. These eyewitnesses did not merely set going a process of oral transmission that soon went its own way without reference to them. They remained throughout their lifetimes the sources and, in some sense that may have varied for figures of central or more marginal significance, the authoritative guarantors of the stories they continued to tell.[19]

In the minds of "form critics," who prefer amorphous groups to historic personalities, the idea of "the creative community" diverts attention from all such "concrete traditionists."[20] But the Swedish scholar Birger Gerhardsson, holding form criticism to be overrated, gave special weight to the "authoritative collegium" of the Twelve.[21]

> If [the Twelve] were close companions of Jesus throughout his ministry, as the Gospels claim they were, and if they were also, as most scholars agree, the first leaders of the mother church in Jerusalem and of its initial outreach elsewhere, we should certainly expect them to have been authoritative transmitters of the traditions of Jesus and to have had something like an official status for their formulations of those traditions.[22]

That common oral preaching will have included much that modern investigators would be happy to call "biographical," since the words and actions of the central figure of the preaching were inevitably key to introducing his claims.

Once the materials of the apostolic preaching were re-expressed in written form, they gave rise to a subset of ancient biographical writing. These will be our Gospels. As Graham Stanton explains, in such writing

> there was a deeply rooted conviction that a person's actions and words sum up the character of an individual more adequately than the comments of an observer. The evangelists rarely intrude into their narratives in order to explain directly to the reader the significance of what has been said or done.[23]

Reports on the provenance of the Gospel books made available by the Church's earliest historians bear no relation to the models of literary production on which form criticism relies.[24] The models on which form critics base themselves are drawn from folk cultures with low literacy levels—not a helpful range of comparison for Roman Palestine—and they presume the slow gestation of texts over long periods of time, time which, in the Gospels' case, is simply unavailable.

So a common oral tradition is key background for the Gospels. Appeal to such tradition need not exclude some attempt to suggest the order of writing of the Gospels. For the early sub-apostolic witness of Clement of Alexandria, the order of composition of the four runs first Matthew, then Luke, then Mark, then John. It is an ordering which, since its revival in nineteenth-century Germany, has commended itself to a number of present-day exegetes. It avoids explanations of any one of the Synoptic Gospels that turns on hypothetical source documents no longer available—if they ever were. And it points to a shared conviction of the early historians: namely, the special importance of *St. Matthew* in the quest for Jesus.

Among the ancient writers of the generation or two following the apostles, there is a multiply sourced report that the Gospel of Matthew existed at some point in a Semitic language, whether that were Hebrew or Aramaic.[25] In his civil career, as collector of taxes, Matthew had been a professional notetaker, listening in Aramaic and writing in Greek. He was doing so on a complex topic—so much so that many tax collectors saw the value of learning shorthand, the use of which was widespread in the Graeco-Roman world, as was the carrying of notebooks. It is perfectly thinkable that Jesus "observed the faith and commitment of Levi the tax-collector and recognized him as one who was capable of making a record of his teaching."[26] It would certainly explain the prominence given to the call of Matthew in the Synoptic Gospels. Of the incidents of personal callings in the Synoptic tradition, St. Matthew is the only example of an apostle whose call narrative is presented but who was not himself a major figure—not a major figure, that is, unless he wrote a Gospel book and the first Gospel book at that.

> In the case of his own gospel, it could be the author modestly stating his credentials. Similarly Mark and Luke were recalling the credentials of the man who had no distinction in the church except for one thing: he had given the world his magnificent book—and that would have made him of interest to all Christian readers.[27]

What, then, does Matthew's Gospel book report? After he has finished with the infancy narratives, Matthew adopts the order that the common catechesis had possessed from the beginning. Here one can consult the summaries of the sermons of St. Peter and St. Paul in the Acts of the Apostles (10:37–38, 13:25). Peter and the others, used to giving an account orally to visitors to Jerusalem, naturally began to produce a common outline. Matthew would have followed broadly the chronology it offered, perhaps bringing forward the preaching of the Sermon on the Mount and the conferring of a mission on the Twelve, with a view to underlining the importance of these two events.

Acting and speaking are equally important for the Matthaean Jesus. The opening of Matthew's Gospel book is followed by a series of episodes devoted to the "deeds of the Christ" (11:2). These happenings themselves furnish a running commentary on Jesus's words—on five key discourses, the principal blocks of teaching material Matthew has to transmit. Those five discourses are, first, the moral charter of the Kingdom, 5:1–7:27; second, the instructions to the apostles sent on mission, 9:36–11:1; third, the parables of the Kingdom, 13:1–13:53; fourth, the practice of the Christian virtues, 18:1–19:1; fifth, the Last Things, 24:1–26:1. The works which, so to say, comment on these discourses are "marvels of power, but also of goodness and wisdom," signs, that "make known well enough in him who accomplishes them the Chosen One of God, the Messiah foretold by the prophets, the King of the new Kingdom."[28] The investiture of the Messiah at his Baptism in the Jordan is thus followed by his "manifestation" in Galilee (according to prophecy, this is where the messianic "light" was to shine, Isaiah 8:23–9:1), before he lays the foundations of his Church on the Galilaean "periphery," and undertakes his climactic ministry in Jerusalem.[29] Stories of the doings of the Messiah, presumably in regular use by the apostles in their preaching work, are thus prefaced to the ultimate "deed of the Christ," described as this in the narrative of his Passion and Resurrection. Once the notion of putting into writing a comprehensive account of the Jesus narrative was floated, St. Matthew would surely have accorded priority to the Paschal events.

A fundamental chronology of broadly this kind is common to the Synoptic Gospels. First come the episodes that make up "the beginning of the preaching of Jesus" (Mark 1:1); that is, the witness of St. John the Precursor and the recalling of the prophecies, the Baptism of Jesus and the witness of the Father that made it a "theophany," this being followed by the Temptations. Then, as the Galilean phase of the ministry unfolds, the confession of Peter brings about a change of orientation to Jerusalem, place of the Passion, as the Passion and its outcome are anticipated in the moment of Jesus's Transfiguration. Lastly, there are the final days before the Triumphal Entry on Palm Sunday, and the Passion and Resurrection events that are the Entry's sequel. This does not rule out the possibility of other, shorter, sequences of events in one or another Gospel book that, precisely as sequences, are historically well founded. Richard Bauckham points out sequences of this sort with special reference to the Gospel according to St. Mark, and this leads me—hereby departing from the Clementine order—to concentrate, after Matthew, on Mark's own book.

In the Passion narrative of St. Mark's Gospel, comments Bauckham, "there are many episodes that, for causal or chronological reasons, necessarily belong in the sequence that Mark presents."[30] For Bauckham, Mark's narrative, with its repetitious "And after that . . ." formula, corresponds to oral procedures, the kind of exposition that might be expected in word-of-mouth delivery, ignoring more sophisticated rhetorical forms of the kind found in writing.[31] This strengthens the case for Mark's dependence on the preaching of Peter, affirmed as it is by the ancient authorities. Mark's Gospel book reads like the performance in writing of a story originally told by word of mouth. Deliberately, if discreetly, Mark draws attention to the special significance of the apostle Peter, doing so by means of the literary device called "inclusion." The first disciple named in the gospel book is Simon (i.e., Peter). The evangelist then repeats Peter's name as if drumming it into our ears right from the start ("Simon and Simon's brother," 3:16). And, creating the "inclusion," Mark ends his book by drawing attention to Peter once again. This is in Mark's Resurrection narrative where the women at the tomb are given a message for Jesus's "disciples and Peter"(16:7)—even though, of course, Peter *is* one of the disciples anyway. St. Mark mentions Peter by name much more often than St. Matthew does (despite Matthew's recording Jesus's commissioning of Peter as the "rock" on which his Church will be built).[32] The striking use of detail in Mark is best thought of not as literary ingenuity but as vivid touches from an eyewitness; John Wenham calls them, quite openly, "Petrine recollections."[33]

On the "Clementine" view I have commended, Mark's book is specifically the *third* gospel in order of writing, and only the *second* by canonical order. Its genesis as a Petrine by-product is readily explicable if this is so.

Peter had found himself caught in crossfire between the hardline Torah party and the supporters of Paul, and the tension had been aggravated first by the publication of Matthew's gospel and then of Luke-Acts. When he came to Rome [again] in the mid-60s, he took no sides, commending both gospels as being representative of apostolic teaching. After the death of Peter and Paul the Romans turned to Mark, who had worked with both apostles, and asked for a record of Peter's teaching. Being a practical people they wanted the bedrock message. Taking Peter's public speeches as his guide and model and making no attempt to be innovative, he got to work on the two gospels. He wove their accounts into a composite narrative, "paragraph by paragraph, sentence by sentence, and even word by word."[34]

It is an objection to the Clementine order that St. Irenaeus, a second century Church Father, placed Mark *before* Luke. But the—in itself, perfectly natural—assumption that Irenaeus is talking about the chronological order of composition of the Gospels may not be correct.

[T]he reason for mentioning Mark and Luke in that order may have arisen simply because [Irenaeus] has just mentioned Peter and Paul and his desire is to "establish that these two apostles are also to be credited with gospels through their close associates."[35]

St. Luke is as much associated with St. Paul on his missionary journeys as St. Mark is with St. Peter at Rome.

It is time to give St. Luke's book its due. The preface to Luke's Gospel bulks large in all discussion of the historicity of the material about Jesus in the New Testament.

Luke claims, in accordance with an interpretation widely favoured by the fathers, to have been a follower of all the apostles, probably having lived in Jerusalem for a considerable time in the 40s. He became an expert in the oral traditions which they formulated and authorised, and it is these that he has written up accurately for his patron, Theophilus.[36]

Yet Luke's verb for transmitting data is compatible with written sources as well. The date of Luke's Gospel-book would appear to be set by II Corinthians 8:18, where Paul refers to "the brother whom all the churches praise on account of the gospel." In context this makes Luke, of all pertinent individual "brothers," the most likely candidate. Assuming that Luke's Gospel book must have circulated in the churches of Greece for a year or two at least in order to warrant Paul's remark, a date of around 54 in the Common Era will be arrived at for the completion of the evangelist's work.[37] Yet despite Luke's avowed commitment to a Gospel based on eyewitness sources, the claim has been made that much of his book is the result of sheer imagination created from nothing historical—notably in what regards his "Infancy Gospel" (chapters 1 to 2) and the set of twenty parables, many of them not known from elsewhere, which dominate the central section of his Gospel. These claims can, however, be countered. It has been shown that the nuances of grammar and style in the Infancy Gospel make sense as a

> very wooden, literal translation of Hebrew or Aramaic into Greek . . . not of the type that lends itself to conscious imitation by one who might want to give his writing a biblical (i.e. Old Testament) flavour, since they involve the frequency and usage of various prepositions, articles, adverbs and adjectives rather than more readily reproducible vocabulary or parts of speech. [38]

Again, it has been found that the Lucan parables arrange themselves into a pattern of "inverted parallelism," which was a common device for assisting memory in antiquity. This suggests that this group of parables come from a *remembered*, and therefore a *transmitted*, source.

Outside the trio of the Synoptic evangelists there stands the remaining Gospel book in the New Testament, the Gospel according to St. John. Ancient authorities always place John's Gospel compositionally—as well as canonically—fourth. Surely, then, it must be regarded then as a "late" text? The lateness in question is much mitigated, however, by the Anglican scholar-bishop John A. T. Robinson. Robinson found in this Gospel book early witness that was supplemented afterward by further theological reflection. [39] This may be, in different respects, both the latest and the earliest Gospel we have. Robinson's thesis does not presuppose Johannine authorship. Yet authorship of the Fourth Gospel by John son of Zebedee is perfectly plausible. Modern students, unwilling to believe in a fisherman-author, are misled by false analogies with societies dominated by a knowledge class of liberal professionals. The world has not been ever thus. Moreover, ascribing authorship of the Gospel to the apostle John

> in no way excludes the services of a secretary, or rather of a group of the faithful of which perhaps Aristion and John the Elder formed part, putting into writing, under [John the apostle's] supervision, the recitations of the old master before affirming of them at the end of the work, the apostolic origin and the truth.

With the final words of this citation, de Grandmaison alludes to a verse in the closing section of the Fourth Gospel: "This is the disciple who is bearing witness to these things, and has written these things, and we know that his testimony is true (John 21: 24)." [40] The "Aristion" and "John the Elder" who are named here are shadowy figures sometimes mentioned as possible ghost-writers of this Gospel book. They were "disciples of the Lord" still passing on oral tradition to people known by the sub-apostolic witness Papias of

Hierapolis, himself born around the year 70 and writing, it may be, as early as the year 90.[41]

De Grandmaison has a plausible reconstruction of St. John's career, finding him to be in turn was apostolic writer in the Letters, prophetic seer in the Apocalypse and, finally, as his "colleagues" left the scene by martyrdom, doctrinal evangelist.

Early manuscript evidence lends support to his claim for the unity of the "Johannine corpus."[42] De Grandmaison goes on to say of John's Gospel book itself,

> In particular, the elevation, the singular originality at depth, notwithstanding the rather verbal contact with ambient philosophical thought; the irreducible Semitism of thought flowing in categories that Hellenism and the Oriental religions had elaborated; the fundamentally popular language but exempt from the barbarism that characterises the earlier and more personal booklet of the Apocalypse; the adversaries clearly described in the First Letter sunk here onto a secondary level; the Synoptics known in their substance but scarcely utilised in a literary way, completed, interpreted with authority; the revelation of the Master disengaged from shadows and, so to speak, from the tongues of human conversation: these traits, are they not the ones we could expect from a major witness, independent, disciple and friend of Jesus?[43]

And if we require more convincing of Johannine authorship of the Fourth Gospel, there has to be some explanation of the absence of opposition to this "Spiritual Gospel"—as Clement of Alexandria called it—on its promulgation in churches already in possession of one or more of the Synoptic Gospels, which were so much more like each other than any of them were like this newcomer. The identification of the author as an apostle—the Apostle John—is the best available explanation we have for its smooth process of acceptance.[44]

Certainly the Gospel of John, though far more similar to the other three than to any other ancient document, *does* differ strikingly from the rest of the Gospel books. It does *not* do so, however, in a way that necessarily impugns the historical reliability either of John's own text or of the Synoptic tradition to which that text is related but which it does not mirror.

John's Gospel book furnishes additional historical and topographical information—no longer regarded, in the manner once was *de rigueur*, as thinly disguised symbolism. That information would include examples of sequences of events, such as Bauckham ascribed to St. Mark. The Israel-based Benedictine archeologist Bargil Pixner writes in just those terms of St. John's chronology when it comes to the period immediately preceding his Passion Narrative:

"[S]everal events intervened between [Jesus's] arrival [from Bethany beyond the Jordan] on the Mount of Olives and the festal entry: the resurrection of Lazarus (John 11:1–44), the banning of Jesus; activity by the Sanhedrin (John 11:47–52), Jesus' hiding in the village of Ephraim (present-day Taibeh) on the edge of the desert (John 11:54) and the anointing in Bethany (John 12:1–9). Only then, according to John's Gospel, [there] followed the messianic entrance into the Holy City. All these events are chronologically feasible and in no way contradict the Synoptics."[45]

And indeed,

John seems to know a fair cross-section of the material found in the Synoptics, including uniquely Matthean and Lukan traditions, and he assumes a fair amount of knowledge of that "core kerygma" on the part of his audience. This alone can account for the number of people, places, and events John describes in ways that presuppose information otherwise attested in one or more of the first three Gospels. It also provides one of the major explanations for why he did or did not include various material in his own Gospel.[46]

Good reasons can usually be found for John's omission of much material found in the earlier Gospels. If, for instance, one asks why St. John excludes the narrative parables that are so numerous and prominent in the Synoptic Gospels, an answer is forthcoming.

Given that there was an element of opacity to the parables even for Jewish audiences . . . , that the details which were most immediately intelligible typically involved life in rural Galilee, and that John omits almost all of Jesus' Galilean ministry during which the vast majority of these parables were spoken, we should not be quite as surprised that he omits all of the major, narrative parables. . . . That John was writing to a predominantly Hellenistic Christian audience in a strongly Graeco-Roman environment probably has a lot to do with his omission of this specific form.[47]

That is not to say that St. John's Jesus *never* speaks in narrative parable mode. Consider, for instance, the manner of introduction of the Good Shepherd discourse in John 10:1–5, a little, telling story about thieves and sheepfolds.

But what of the absence, though, in John's Gospel of the literary form—so common in the Synoptics—of the "pronouncement story," otherwise termed the "controversy story"? Unlike the narrative parable, a *chreia* (as the Greeks called it) was perfectly familiar to Hellenistic culture. Craig Blomberg, the author just cited, has an answer here as well.

That John consistently records longer accounts of the controversies Jesus' teaching generated may suggest that he is closer to preserving the outline of an entire dialogue rather than condensing the material into such short and stylized forms as do the Synoptics.[48]

Again, Blomberg proposes that St. John has no exorcism accounts because he wants to present Jesus' *entire life and death* as the overthrow of Satan. This can be paralleled by the suggestion (not Blomberg's) that John omits the Transfiguration episode because he sees his *entire narrative* in the light of the Glory of the Son. Compare what he says in his Prologue: "[A]nd we saw his glory" (John 1:14). In Arthur Michael Ramsey's words, "The Transfiguration is omitted, for the glory belongs not to any isolated episodes but to the story as a whole."[49] That is quite compatible with the thought (this time from Blomberg again) that John was reluctant to include the Transfiguration event for a liturgical reason. The theophany on Mount Hermon (or Mount Thabor) did not tie in so easily with the Jewish festivals on which John has structured much of his Gospel book.[50]

The seeming conflict between the dating of Jesus's cleansing of the Temple in John and the Synoptic Gospels is an obvious difficulty for "additive harmonisation." But it is not an insuperable one. There could well have been a protest by Jesus against the commercialization of the Temple cult at the start of his ministry and a prediction of the end of the sacrificial system near the ministry's close.

> A protest merely against corrupt trade (an enacted fulfillment of Zechariah 14:21) fits better early on in Christ's ministry; the synoptic account, in contrast, seems to threaten the destruction of the entire sacrificial system. The latter, more serious threat almost certainly would have led to Jesus' arrest (Mark 11:18). John's characteristic comments about what the disciples came to understand only after Jesus' resurrection (vv. 17, 22) further supports the idea that John is not blurring distinctions between separate periods in Jesus' ministry here.[51]

The structure of St. John's Gospel is at least as carefully thought through as that of St. Matthew, the main lines of which were presented above. After the Prologue, which could be considered a new version of Beginning-of-the-Gospel-Statements in Matthew and Mark, John's Gospel includes in chapters 2 to 11 seven main signs and seven related discourses (compare Matthew's five blocks of teaching commented on by "deeds"), while chapters 12 to 21 of his book cover the testimony of his Death and Resurrection, corresponding in position, of course, to the equivalent narratives in all three Synoptic Gospels. Blomberg interprets John 2 to 4 as presenting four episodes, none of them found in the Synoptics, which show Jesus's ministry bringing a new joy (the marriage feast at Cana), a new temple (the cleansing), a new birth (the encounter with Nicodemus), and a new offer of salvation (the meeting with the Woman of Samaria), with John 5 to 11 focussing on the relation between

Jesus and four Jewish festivals: Sabbath, Passover, Tabernacles, and Dedication (Hannukah), adding matter not in the Synoptics and connected with visits to Jerusalem for the great feasts.

As to the latter, the Johannine scholar Raymond Brown remarks,

> It is quite plausible . . . that Jesus may have spoken publicly on the occasion of Jewish feasts and may have directed his remarks to a contrast between his own ministry and the theme of the feast. [52]

That is not to say that every word the Savior speaks in the Fourth Gospel can be taken as his *ipsissima verba*. Craig Blomberg is a good guide in the task of distinguishing between strictly historical material in the Fourth Gospel and theological commentary by the evangelist. "[T]he situation-specific circumstances of material ascribed [in John's Gospel] to first-century characters distinguish it from John's free theological summaries that reflect a more cosmic perspective."[53] The use of the solemnization formula "Amen, amen, I say to you" in this Gospel is also contributory in alerting readers to exactly reproduced sayings by Jesus rather than passages more affected by theological amplification. And Blomberg adds,

> Further distinctives emerge because of John's desire to contextualize the Gospel for the Christians in his specific audience [late first century Ephesian Christians challenged by local synagogues] and the concerns they face, as well as from his more dramatic form of the larger literary genre of theological biography. [54]

Raymond Brown asked,

> Does all this mean that the fourth evangelist took Jesus' simple message and reinterpreted it in terms of the O[ld] T[estament] Wisdom literature and of Pharisaic and sectarian thought, perhaps because the evangelist himself was particularly familiar with that thought? Or were such elements already in Jesus' own outlook and expression, and were they to some extent lost in the Synoptic tradition of his works and words?

He replied to his own question:

> A nuanced answer would, in part, include both suggestions. On the one hand, it is time to liberate ourselves from the assumption that Jesus' own thought and expression were always simply and always in one style, and that anything that smacks of theological sophistication must come from the (implicitly more intelligent) evangelists. On the other hand, we must recognize in the fourth evangelist a man of theological genius who has put something of himself and of his own outlook into the composition of the Gospel. . . . Perhaps one key to this problem is the Gospel's own claim to be dependent on the testimony of a

disciple who was particularly loved by Jesus. . . . If this is true, a certain connaturality of thought between disciple and master might be presumed.[55]

The Gospel of John spends much more time on Jesus' formal discourses in synagogue or Temple. It is entirely reasonable to contrast with this the Synoptic Gospels, which focus on his open-air addresses to the crowds. There is also the fact that much more space is given to private utterances to the disciples, above all in chapters 13 to 17, the "Last Supper Discourse" or "High Priestly Prayer." It is sometimes said that the Johannine Jesus speaks in exactly the same manner as the author of the Fourth Gospel does—which, if true, would be suspicious. But careful examination has shown that almost one hundred and fifty different words used by Jesus in St. John's Gospel are never found in the evangelist's own narrative passages.[56]

Summing up on John's testimony, when compared with that of Matthew, Mark, and Luke, Craig Blomberg writes,

> [H]owever exalted John's view of Jesus may seem, it contains nothing which is not implicit in the picture painted by Matthew, Mark and Luke of a man who would sovereignly overrule Jewish interpretations of the Law, claim that his words would last forever, pronounce the forgiveness of sins, describe humanity's eternal destiny as dependent on its reaction to him, demand absolute loyalty from his disciples, offer rest for the weary and salvation for the lost, promise to be with his followers always, and guarantee that God would grant them any prayers requested in his name.[57]

NOTES

1. Graham Stanton, *Gospel Truth? Today's Quest for Jesus of Nazareth* (London: Collins, 1997, 2nd edition), 48.

2. Vincent Taylor, *The Formation of the Gospel Tradition* (London: Macmillan, 1933, 2nd edition), 41–43.

3. Harry Y. Gamble, *Books and Readers in the Early Church: A History of Early Christian Texts* (New Haven: Yale University Press, 1995), 58–65.

4. In the chronology carefully argued by John A. T. Robinson, the Letters to the Philippians, to Philemon, to the Colossians, the Ephesians, and the Second Letter to Timothy are all dated to the year 58. See John A. T. Robinson, *Redating the New Testament* (London: SCM Press, 1976), 84. Though calling his findings "tentative," Robinson explains that by that adjective he means simply they may be "a year out either way."

5. John Wenham, *Redating Matthew, Mark and Luke. A Fresh Assault on the Synoptic Problem* (London: Hodder and Stoughton, 1991), 217.

6. David L. Dungan, *The Sayings of Jesus in the Churches of Paul* (Philadelphia: Fortress, 1971).

7. See also David Wenham, *Paul: Follower of Jesus or Founder of Christianity?* (Grand Rapids, MI: Eerdmans, 1995).

8. Craig L. Blomberg, *The Historical Reliability of the Gospels* (Leicester: Inter-Varsity Press, 1987), 222.

9. Léonce de Grandmaison, S. J., *Jésus Christ, Sa personne, son message, ses oeuvres* (Paris: Beauchesne, 1928, 2nd edition), I., 34.

10. Richard Bauckham, *Jesus and the Eyewitnesses. The Gospels as Eyewitness Testimony* (Grand Rapids, MI: Eerdmans, 2006), 266–67.

11. Léonce de Grandmaison, S. J., *Jésus Christ*, I., 34.

12. Léonce de Grandmaison, S. J., *Jésus* Christ, 29–30.

13. John Wenham, *Redating Matthew, Mark and Luke*, 220.

14. Larry W. Hurtado, *One God, One Lord: Early Christian Devotion and Ancient Jewish Monotheism* (London: Bloomsbury T & T Clark, 2015, 3rd edition), 4.

15. Hurtado, *One God, One* Lord, 4.

16. Léonce de Grandmaison, S. J., *Jésus Christ*, I., 101.

17. John Wenham, *Redating Matthew, Mark and Luke*, 77.

18. Larry W. Hurtado, *Lord Jesus Christ. Devotion to Jesus in Earliest Christianity* (Grand Rapids, MH, and Cambridge: Eerdmans, 2005), 196.

19. Richard Bauckham, *Jesus and the Eyewitnesses*, 93.

20. Birger Gerhardsson, *The Reliability of the Gospel Tradition* (Peabody, MA: Hendrickson, 2001), 74.

21. Gerhardsson, *The Reliability of the Gospel Tradition*, 73.

22. Richard Bauckham, *Jesus and the Eyewitnesses*, 94.

23. Graham Stanton, *Gospel Truth?*, 139.

24. See, in particular, the fragmentarily surviving *Exposition of the Oracles of the Lord* by Papias of Hierapolis, a friend of Polycarp of Smyrna. Though the writers who transmit the surviving fragments of this work, (Irenaeus and Eusebius) disagree as to whether Papias, like Polycarp, also knew the apostle John, his text has been described as taking a form that is "very ancient and closely associated with the apostolic era," Hubertus R. Drobner, *The Fathers of the Church. A Comprehensive Introduction* (Peabody, MA: Hendrickson, 2007), 55.

25. For authorities from the Greek, Syriac, Coptic and Latin traditions of the sub-apostolic and patristic periods, see Marie-Joseph Lagrange, O. P., *Evangile selon saint Matthieu* (Paris: Gabalda, 1948, 8th edition), XI–XV.

26. John Wenham, *Redating Matthew, Mark and Luke*, 112.

27. Wenham, *Redating Matthew, Mark and Luke*, 113–14.

28. Léonce de Grandmaison, *Jésus Christ*, I. 67.

29. Marie-Joseph Lagrange, O. P., *Evangile selon saint Matthieu*, XXV.

30. Richard Bauckham, *Jesus and the Eyewitnesses*, 230.

31. Bauckham, *Jesus and the Eyewitnesses*, 233, citing Joanna Dewey, "The Survival of Mark's Gospel: a Good Story?" *Journal of Biblical Literature* 123 (2004), 495–507, and here at 499.

32. Richard Bauckham, *Jesus and the Eyewitnesses*, 124–26.

33. Cited John Wenham, *Redating Matthew, Mark and Luke,* 180, from H. D. A. Major, *Recollections of Jesus by an Eye-Witness* (London: Murray, 1925).

34. John Wenham, *Redating Matthew, Mark and Luke,* 16, citing David Dungan, "The Purpose and Provenance of the Gospel of Mark according to the Two-Gospel (Owen-Griesbach) Hypothesis," in W. R. Farmer (ed.), *New Synoptic Studies* (Macon: Mercer University Press, 1983), 414. It should be noted, though, that for the account (preserved in Eusebius) of the origin of the Gospel book by Clement of Alexandria, a church which according to the Coptic tradition was founded by Mark himself, publication preceded Peter's death, rather than following it.

35. John Wenham, *Redating Matthew, Mark, Luke*, 191, citing W. R. Farmer (ed.), *New Synoptic Studies*, 12.

36. John Wenham, *Redating Matthew, Mark and Luke*, 7–8.

37. Wenham, *Redating Matthew, Mark and Luke*, 236.

38. Craig L. Blomberg, *The Historical Reliability of the Gospels*, 17.

39. John A. T. Robinson, *The Priority of John* (London: SCM, 1985).

40. Léonce de Grandmaison, *Jésus Christ*, I. p. 184. Richard Bauckham, however, understands the "we" here as the "we" of "authoritative testimony," and takes it as equivalent to the "I" of the Beloved Disciple himself, the author of the Gospel, see *Jesus and the Eyewitnesses*, 369–83.

41. For a detailed discussion see De Grandmaison, *Jésus Christ*, 15–21.

42. See Charles E. Hill, *The Johannine Corpus in the Early Church* (Oxford: Oxford University Press, 2004).

43. Léonce de Grandmaison, *Jésus Christ*, I., 186. De Grandmaison would of course have introduced a reference to the Qumran writings in this description of Semitic thought in Greek and Oriental categories had he lived after the discovery of the Dead Sea Scrolls.

44. Léonce de Grandmaison, *Jésus Christ*, p. 187.

45. Bargil Pixner, O. S. B., *With Jesus through Galilee according to the Fifth Gospel* (Rosh Pina: Corazin Publishing, 1992), 113.

46. Craig L. Blomberg, *The Historical Reliability of John's Gospel: Issues and Commentary* (IVP Academic Press, Downers Grove, IL, 2002), 284.

47. Blomberg, *The Historical Reliability of John's Gospel*, 50. For that "opacity" Blomberg directs his readers to Mark 4:11–12 and parallels.

48. Blomberg, *The Historical Reliability of John's Gospel*, 51.

49. Arthur Michael Ramsey, *The Glory of God and the Transfiguration of Christ* (London: Darton, Longman and Todd, 1967 [1949]), 57.

50. Craig L. Blomberg, *The Historical Reliability of John's Gospel*, 55.

51. Blomberg, *The Historical Reliability of John's Gospel*, 90–91.

52. Raymond E. Brown, S. S., *The Gospel according to John [i–xii]* (London, Chapman, 1971), XLIX.

53. Craig L. Blomberg, *The Historical Reliability of John's Gospel*, 98.

54. Blomberg, *The Historical Reliability of John's Gospel*, 285.

55. Raymond E. Brown, S. S., *The Gospel according to John [i–xii]*, LXIV.

56. Craig L. Blomberg, *The Historical Reliability of the Gospels*, 183.

57. Blomberg, *The Historical Reliability of John's Gospel*, 166.

Chapter Two

Christ

So much for the chief witnesses; now it is time to attempt, on the basis of the content of their testimony, a "Christology"—a theologically informed portrait of Jesus Christ.

As the New Testament authors present him, Jesus of Nazareth fulfilled the hope of Israel for a person who would actualize the Old Testament promises of God, though he did so in a way none of the biblical writers had thought of: namely, by uniting in himself four very different sorts of prophecy about "He who is Coming." Looking back at his volume on the Old Testament in his theological aesthetics, *The Glory of the Lord*, Hans Urs von Balthasar explained:

> At the end of the preceding volume, we offered a new formulation of the *argumentum ex prophetia*: the numerous images of the Old Testament surround and converge upon a midpoint which remains open and not constructible; through the existence of Christ this midpoint is occupied, without visible struggling to attain the synthesis; as Christians reflect on this after Easter, it is seen that all fragmentary images order themselves as if automatically towards this midpoint, and contribute a clarification to the unity.[1]

Hebrew and Greek words for "fulfil" have a broader reference than their English counterparts. Brevard Childs, the founder of "Canon Criticism" (a deliberate reading of one biblical text in the context of all the rest) wrote, "A word is fulfilled when it is filled full to form a whole."[2] "The Hebrew concept is naïve. An event is fulfilled when it is full. One determines it by its content, and when it is full, it evidences by itself the fullness."[3] The admirable Blomberg concurs:

In one sense all the Old Testament is self-consciously incomplete, looking
forward to the time when God would save his people once and for all. Thus
Jesus can speak of his fulfilling all Scripture (Matthew 5:17; Luke 24: 27), as a
whole, without implying that every individual sentence in the [Old Testament]
was meant to describe some facet of the Messiah's ministry.[4]

According him the title "Christos" was not a later invention: that Jesus saw
himself as the Messiah is a perfectly defensible reading of the Gospel evidence.[5] But what kind of Messiah is the question. Not one that any single Old
Testament author had ever envisaged. The Anglican theologian Austin Farrer
put this strikingly not to say brutally:

Jesus Christ clothed himself in all the images of messianic promise, and in
living them out crucified them; but the crucified reality is better than the
figures of prophecy.[6]

What were these figures? There were predictions based on the Zion theology of the Psalter and on the prophetic movement in the Southern Kingdom
(Judah) about a triumphant king-to-come of David's line. There were apocalyptic prophecies about a new form of God's own presence, signaled in
dramatic shifts, registered in visionary mode, in the angelic realm. Thus in
the Book of Daniel the "Ancient of Days" receives at his side an angelic
figure, Israel's vindicator, "like a son of man" (7:13). There were prophecies,
this time of enormous antiquity in Israel, about a great teacher to come, a
"Prophet-like-Moses." And there were prophecies deriving from the Isaianic
corpus about a "Suffering Servant" whom God would exalt. The absolute
originality of Jesus as a figure in history is that he not only claimed to be the
synthesis of these four quite heterogeneous visions of the future by the seers
of Israel, accepting in different manners, whether tacit or explicit, and whether earlier or later in his short career, the titles of King or Shepherd, Son of
Man, Prophet or Teacher, and Servant. More than that, he showed he actually
was that synthesis in and through the events of his life, death, and Resurrection. He demonstrated how he was a glorious King, supreme Prophet, self-
sacrificing Servant, and the transcendentally originated Man, in the Paschal
Mystery by which he consummated the hope of Israel. Retrospectively, as
Balthasar argues, all becomes plain:

Looking backwards from the fulfillment in Christ, it is possible to show that it
was precisely this form alone that corresponded to the postulates, but likewise,
that this form could never have been rounded out to fullness from the fragments which were available to the old covenant. The fullness was not present
in the fragments in the way that the fullness of a jigsaw is present in the pieces,
too hard for a child who needs the help of an adult to fit them together; the
fullness here came about only through a synthesis possible for God alone, yet
absolutely undiscoverable for man. In spite of which the fullness was present

in the parts in such a way that man could recognize it subsequently, though in this act of recognition he had to acknowledge it as the sole work of God in history.[7]

He also left his community with a task of theological construction that they carried out by naming him the Father's Son, come in human flesh—or as the later doctrinal formulation will have it, God and man, his two natures united in a single Person. In this they could rely on his promise of "another Paraclete" (John 14:16), the Holy Spirit whom he would send from the Father. For Old Testament thinking,

> [i]t was impossible for man alone in his intercession and his suffering for others to establish God's own and entire righteousness upon earth: but it was likewise impossible for God's *dabar* [Word] alone to take this upon itself, for he cannot bypass or overtrump the God-given freedom of man (the freedom which ennobles him to be the image of God): but this could be achieved by a form which was the absolute identity of God's Word and a man who in free obedience took on himself the sin, now not merely of the people, but of the world. In his atoning death, judgment and mercy came together, so that the final judgment that should bring doom became a function of the final mercy that wished to establish God's new and eternal covenant with the world. From the standpoint of the old covenant, this identification of the two pillars remains unthinkable, for it appears to take away the fundamental principle on which everything is built, namely the infinite qualitative difference between God and creature. Even when this identification has taken place, it remains a mystery that is never to be fully laid bare, yet that by the force of its existence casts a wholly new light on God himself and on his relationship to the world: on God, because the mystery of the God-man necessarily discloses the mystery of the Trinity within the Godhead. The light falls on God's relationship to the world, for now, without encroachment upon the difference between God and creature, the world can find in the life of the Trinity its allotted space. It is only by looking backwards from the new covenant that any of these considerations became possible.[8]

There thus fell to the community of the Messiah a twofold task: to think through the issue of who the Christ is (Christology), and to adjust, accordingly, the doctrine of God (Triadology, thinking about the Holy Trinity).

How did the Church the apostles left behind go on to produce Christological doctrine basing itself on such Scriptural witness? Doing so was the great contribution of the Church Fathers and the first seven Councils of the Church, those assemblies Catholics recognize, together with the Eastern Orthodox, as answering two very basic questions. First, how does the divinity of Christ square with the monotheism of Israel, which monotheism is also a postulate of good philosophy, when it puts forward the proposition that there is only one God? And secondly, how is the assertion of Christ's divinity compatible with the testimony of the New Testament that Jesus was at the same time one of us, a man—albeit with a unique human role, comprising within itself the tasks of Shepherd-King, supreme Prophet, self-sacrificing or "priestly" Servant, and "Danielic" Vindicator, all of which were necessary if the hope of Israel was to be fulfilled in his person.

We can state the contribution of the Seven Councils succinctly in their proper sequence. The First Council of Nicaea, 325, taught that in his divinity Jesus Christ is "consubstantial" with the Father: that is, the Father generates him by communicating to him his own substance, the unique divine nature. The First Council of Constantinople, 381, by affirming the divinity of the Holy Spirit that the Son sent from the Father at Pentecost tacitly taught the equality of the Son with the Father since only One who is God exactly as the Father is God can be at the source of sending into the world another divine person, namely the Holy Spirit. The Council of Ephesus, 431, by asserting that blessed Mary is the Mother of God, taught that the instance of our human nature that came to be in her womb has as its personal subject this same divine Son who is co-equal with the Father. The Council of Chalcedon, 451, added that the two natures, the divinity affirmed at the First Council of Nicaea and the humanity affirmed at Ephesus, are united in the single person of the Savior without either confusion or separation. They are not commingled but neither are they in any way disjoined. The Second Council of Constantinople, 553, insisted that this single person spoken of at Chalcedon is not the result of the coming to be of the divinity and humanity in the union between them in Mary's womb but is the selfsame eternally existing divine Son affirmed at Nicaea I. The Third Council of Constantinople, 681, made it clear that in Christ, a divine will and a human will are both present, simultaneously co-energizing in the unity of his single personhood. The Second Council of Nicaea, 787, taught that because the single divine person is operative in the human nature of the Word, showing itself in his human action, it follows that visual images of Jesus, either in himself as in a portrait or as engaged in action, as in narrative art, can be worshipped as images of God himself.

To find the Christology of the Councils expressed in more systematic form, we could turn to St. John of Damascus in the East or, again, to St. Thomas in the West. Both are supreme summators of the Conciliar doctrines. We shall choose the Western doctor here, conscious of his lifelong project of drawing into his *oeuvre* the texts of those councils held in the East and of the Greek fathers, not least Damascene himself.[9]

In the Questions that open the Third (and final) Part of his master work, the *Summa theologiae*, Thomas lays out, with the care for exact expression that never left him, the unique makeup of Christ as the great Councils proclaimed him to be. He explains that Christ is one divine person in whom two natures, the divine nature and our human nature, are perfectly united—united, as the Fourth Ecumenical Council, the Council of Chalcedon, puts it "without confusion or change," the Godhead of the Son remaining what it was but taking our human nature into union with itself, so that he, Jesus, who is born in time in our humanity is also God from all eternity, generated by the Father before all ages: the selfsame person, both God and man, who is never to be considered as "divided or separated into two persons," the Word on the one hand and Christ on the other. That would be quite erroneous since "the union"—so Thomas sums up the true mind of the Fathers and Councils—"took place *in* his person."[10]

Thomas will use his profound philosophy of being—his metaphysics—to underpin the teaching of the Fathers—and especially the teaching of St. Cyril of Alexandria (influential on the Third, Fourth, and Fifth Councils) who so strongly emphasized the unity of the person of Christ as God made man. He will explain that in the Word incarnate there is only one *esse*. This word is at the center of Thomas's philosophy. It is a term that in Latin is both a noun and a verb, and so it is usually translated not "a being"—which, if the term were only a noun, could serve well enough—but, rather, "an act of existence," a phrase anyone interested in Thomas's metaphysics needs to investigate.[11] In the Christological context, Thomas is saying in and through this *esse* word that there is only one act in which the God-man has his fully actualized being. If instead we were to speak here of a *two*fold act (as Thomas himself had done, a few years before writing the *Summa* in his "Disputed Question on the Incarnate Word"), it could only be because the single act of existence of Jesus Christ may be understood in two ways: namely, as the act of existence which, in a *primary* sense is proper to the Word who is God, and which, in a *secondary* sense is proper to the human nature of the Word who, insofar as he is a personal subject subsisting in our humanity, is himself a man.[12]

What was the rationale of the union? Why on earth did the Word become incarnate anyway? The very first question of the Third Part of Thomas's *Summa Theologiae* (where his own account of the "deep mysteries" can be found) throws light on this. For the sake of the re-formation of the human race, it was highly fitting that "the Highest Good should communicate itself to the creature in the highest way possible,"[13] namely, by *personal union with our nature*. The amazing intimacy of God to man, which the Lord brought about in the union, could best serve what Thomas calls our "furtherance in good" and also our "deliverance from evil." The contrast he draws between what we need to be formed anew *for* and what we need to be formed anew *from out of* is neatly turned in Latin by two words that match each other in sound: God suitably took a creature into personal union with himself so as to assure humanity's *promotio*—its "promotion"—in good; and also its *remotio*—humanity's "removal"—from evil.[14]

Thomas gives two reasons why it was fitting, *conveniens*, that the Son of God, who is God's Wisdom and Word, should take to himself human nature.[15] The first concerns the "dignity" of that nature. As creatures made by the Wisdom of God to be, in his image, truly intelligent, human beings could be in contact with the divine Word through knowing and loving him, so there is some sort of foundation here for the stupendous Incarnation event. Here, tacitly, the emphasis lies on "furtherance in good" as the Incarnation's rationale. In his (early) *Writing on the Sentences* Thomas thought it probable that for the "glorification," *exaltatio*, of human nature and the "coronation," *consummatio*, of the whole universe, the Incarnation would have taken place even without the Fall.

His second explanation of the appropriateness, *convenientia*, of the Incarnation concerns humanity's radical need for it. Our human nature was in dire need of restoration, of being reformed to the condition of those made in the image of God, for they had lost his likeness.[16] By the time he wrote his *Summa theologiae* Thomas stressed especially this "deliverance from evil," since remedying sin is so much the rationale for the coming of the Saviour that is given in Scripture itself.[17]

In his *Summa contra Gentiles* he had a winning thought that continued to leave its mark on his Christology. The assumption of our nature by One who is divine reanimated the human hope for beatitude and aroused a desire to have the fruition of God through enjoying God's friendship—so much easier to do with God-made-human.[18]

Naturally enough, then, Thomas has to address the *consequences of the union not just for Christ but for humankind*.[19] The grace of union that at the Incarnation joined human nature to the divine nature is utterly unique; yet from it there flowed not only the gifts of grace that filled Christ's human soul from the very start of its existence.[20] From the grace of union came also the gifts of grace that are *offered to other human beings* as the age of salvation unfolds. The assumption of our nature by God the Son is the source of grace for us, since the restoration—the re-formation, or, as is said in more usual religious language, the "salvation"—of the human race depends on it.[21]

In his *Summa theologiae*, St. Thomas goes on to offer a presentation of the story of Christ that unlike the "standard" academic exegete today—or, for that matter, the person who opens the gospels merely casually—presumes throughout his reading the faith of the Councils. Indeed, Thomas does not open his account of the life of Christ until he has reminded his readers of the upshot of that crucial development of doctrine. Here he puts into our hands the essentials of how the Fathers of the Church saw the witness of Scripture to their Redeemer Lord.

What the Fathers have to say about Christ is critical because, as Cardinal Joseph Ratzinger urged in his theological writings, it is only when the biblical revelation enters into the mind and heart of the Fathers of the Church that this revelation is fully registered, completely received, for what it really is.[22] It is for this reason that patristics is a desirable guide to what the Scriptures have to say. Similarly, Thomas regards the truth that the doctrine of the patristic era Councils proclaims as essential for fully appreciating the life of Christ. And that, quite simply, is the first reason why the chief events of that life come across as what I am calling, in the title of this book, "deep mysteries," since the person who was engaged in those events as their subject was himself almighty God.

The principal events of the life of Christ, so it will emerge as the *Summa theologiae* continues its way, are the channels by which he is the source of grace for humans. That is the second reason why, as people celebrate those events in the Church's liturgical year or meditate on them in spiritual reading and prayer, they need to recognize that these are "deep mysteries" with which they have to do. They are deep not only because One who is God is their subject but because they are the means by which he worked out human salvation.

Those events affect people not only when they are thinking about them but throughout their lives, since they provide the "form" (important word) human salvation takes, the shape (so to say) that saving grace takes in Christian existence. That will be the third and climactic reason for calling these mysteries "deep." They are deep not only because One who is God is their subject and not only because they are the means by which he worked out man's salvation but also because they confer an abiding form on Christian lives. Their causal power is not only efficacious, it is exemplary as well. In this, they are simply a unique example (or set of examples) of the overall metaphysical relation of God to the world. In the words of Aquinas,

> Everything found in us comes from God and is linked with him as to its efficient cause and its exemplary cause: he is the efficient cause, since through God's active power everything is accomplished in us; he is the exemplary cause because everything in us which is of God imitates God in some way.[23]

I said that the mysteries' exemplary form is the "shape that saving grace takes in Christian existence." So what is "grace"? Grace is a participation in the divine life in accordance with the purposes the loving mercy of God has for his creatures. But *how* has God done so, how *does* God do so?[24] As God, Christ can give us the Father's grace in his own right, while as man he can and does give that same grace "instrumentally," using his humanity as the instrument of his divinity. He acts upon us *instrumentally* through those saving actions of his that bring about grace in us. It was a conviction he had taken from Damascene's *On the Orthodox Faith*.[25] In the succeeding article of this Question Thomas writes,

> [T]he power of influence of the humanity of Christ comes from its union with the Word of God, to whom the body is joined by means of the soul, as was

established earlier. Hence, the entire humanity of Christ, body and soul, acts upon men, on their bodies as well as on their souls.[26]

Thomas is fully in continuity with the Fathers, translating into a vocabulary more metaphysically alert, if also stripped, their intuitions into the *mysteria Christi*: the *sacramenta* or *exempla* that convey the power of God present to us in "the liturgical, sacramental and preaching life of the church."[27] For "everything in the life, death, and resurrection of Jesus works at the level of *exemplum* (inspiring and exemplifying our response to God's grace) and of *mysterium* or *sacramentum* (empowering and assisting that response)."[28] That is a modern scholar's comment on the doctrine of St. Leo, one of Thomas's sources. Leo helped Aquinas in his *tour de force* in the *Tertia Pars* of the *Summa theologiae*. "Thomas Aquinas was the first (and would remain for a long time the only) theologian to re-group into a coherent and organized whole the *ensemble of the principal events of the life of Christ I*."[29] And the way Thomas did so continues the line of thinking of the patristic pope. Thomas's aim is to "disengage the meaning and the salvific efficacy of each of the acts [of the Word incarnate] in the history of salvation and to set in relief the exemplarity of each of them and of his entire life for Christian living."[30]

If one consults the Liturgy, the Fathers, and the classical theologians such as Thomas, the content of the Gospel, the Good News, the message carried by the Church, is not in doubt. It runs this way: the Father has a plan for adopting human beings as his sons and daughters and this plan will mean their liberation from all ills and their establishment in the highest possible good. He has carried out that plan through his natural Son, his Beloved from all eternity, sending him into the world in our human nature for our salvation. That salvation, seen negatively, is our rescue from a condition of alienation from God through a sacrifice commensurate (and more than commensurate) in value with the disvalue of the wrongs our race has done. So it means forgiveness and reconciliation with God. The same salvation, seen positively, is our entry into the intimacy of the divine life as adopted brothers and sisters of the Father's Only Begotten. So it means eternal life and deification. In itself, salvation "eventualized," actually happened, in the mysteries of the God-man's death and Resurrection. In his Paschal Mystery he realized the roles the prophets had predicted, as suffering Servant in his death, as glorious King in his Resurrection, and he did so with the maximal effect for others that was possible because he was personally God, energizing in the divine nature as well as in our own. In his Crucifixion the Servant made sacrifice for us as sinful creatures, becoming in so doing our Great High Priest. In his Resurrection the triumphant King opened the way for us as creatures made for God into the new realm his Easter victory brought into being; and in his Ascension as the Son of Man—the Vindicator—he took our humanity to the

Father's throne. And throughout, as the Prophet to end all prophets, he gave clear indications of how those roles were to be understood.

NOTES

1. Hans Urs von Balthasar, *The Glory of the Lord: A Theological Aesthetics. VII. The New Covenant* (Edinburgh: T. and T. Clark, 1989), 33–34.
2. Brevard Childs, "Prophecy and Fulfilment: A Study of Contemporary Hermeneutics," *Interpretation* 12 (1958), 259–71, and here at 267.
3. Childs, "Prophecy and Fulfilment," 258. Childs thus supplied the Old Testament grounds for the New Testament interpretation of that fullness in C. H. Dodd's classic study, *According to the Scriptures* (London: Nisbet, 1952).
4. Craig L. Blomberg, *The Historical Reliability of the Gospels*, 52.
5. See for instance Martin Hengel, "Jesus, the Messiah of Israel: The Debate about the "Messianic Mission" of Jesus," in Bruce Chilton and Craig A. Evans (ed.), *Authenticating the Activities of Jesus* (Leiden: Brill, 1999), 323–49.
6. Austin Farrer, "An English Appreciation," in Hans Werner Bartsch (ed.), *Kerygma and Myth: A Theological Debate* (London: SPCK, 1953), 212–23, and here at 223.
7. Hans Urs von Balthasar, *The Glory of the Lord: A Theological Aesthetics. VII. The New Covenant*, 33.
8. Hans Urs von Balthasar, *The Glory of the Lord: A Theological Aesthetics, I: Seeing the Form* (Edinburgh: T. and T. Clark, 1982), 36.
9. His commentary on the Gospels, the *Catena aurea*, "draws on the work of fifty-seven Greek authors as opposed to only twenty-two Latin authors. We can well understand, then, that Thomas regarded himself as the legitimate heir of the Greek Fathers." Jean-Pierre Torrell, O. P., *Saint Thomas Aquinas: Volume 2, Spiritual Master* (Washington, DC: Catholic University of America Press, 2003), 126–27. See also Louis-Jacques Bataillon, O. P., "Saint Thomas et les Pères: De la Catena à la Tertia Pars," in Carlos-Josaphat Pinto da Oliveira (ed.), *Ordo sapientiae et amoris. Image et message de saint Thomas d'Aquin à travers les récentes études historiques, herméneutiques et doctrinales. Hommage au professeur Jean-Pierre Torrell à l'occasion de son 65e anniversaire* (Fribourg: Editions universitaires, 1993), 15–36.
10. Thomas Aquinas, *Summa theologiae*, IIIa., q. 2, a. 5, sed contra. Italics are, of course, added.
11. Aquinas, *Summa theologiae*, IIIa., q. 17, a. 2.
12. I follow here Colman O'Neill, O. P., "Unity of Existence in Christ (3a. 17, 2)," in Colman O'Neill (ed.), *St. Thomas Aquinas, Summa Theologiae, Volume 50: The One Mediator* (London: Eyre and Spottiswoode, 1965), 221–28.
13. Thomas Aquinas, *Summa theologiae*, IIIa., q. 1, a. 1, corpus.
14. Aquinas, *Summa theologiae*, IIIa., q. 1, a. 2, corpus.
15. This language of "fittingness," with its connotations of what is lovely, beautiful, is Thomas's version of theological aesthetics. See Gilbert Narcisse, *Les raisons de Dieu: Argument de convenance et esthétique théologique selon saint Thomas d'Aquin et Hans Urs von Balthasar* (Fribourg: Editions universitaires, 1997).
16. Thomas Aquinas, *Summa theologiae*, IIIa., q. 4, a. 1.
17. Aquinas, *Summa theologiae*, IIIa., q. 1, a. 3. See on this Michel Corbin, "La Parole devenue chair: Lecture de la première question de la *Tertia Pars* de la *Somme théologique* de Thomas d'Aquin," *Revue des sciences philosophiques et théologiques* 67 (1978), 5–40.
18. Thomas Aquinas, *Summa contra Gentiles* IV. 54. For a commentary on this passage, see Jean-Pierre Torrell, O. P., 107–109.
19. Thomas Aquinas, *Summa theologiae* IIIa., q. 2 is devoted to this topic.
20. Aquinas, *Summa theologiae*, IIIa., q. 2, a. 12, corpus.
21. Aquinas, *Summa theologiae*, IIIa., q. 2, a. 11, corpus.

22. Joseph Ratzinger, "Die Bedeutung der Väter im Aufbau des Glaubens," in Joseph Ratzinger, *Theologische Prinzipienlehre: Bausteine zur Fundamentaltheologie* (Munich: Erich Wewel, 1982), 139–58.

23. Thomas Aquinas, *Summa contra Gentiles*, IV. 21.

24. Thomas Aquinas, *Summa theologiae*, IIIa., q. 8, a. 1.

25. John of Damascus, *On the Orthodox Faith*, 59 and 63. Compare Thomas Aquinas, *Summa theologiae* Ia. IIae., q. 112, a. 1, ad i.

26. Aquinas, IIIa., q. 8, a. 2, corpus.

27. J. Mark Armitage, *A Twofold Solidarity: Leo the Great's Theology of Redemption* (Strathfield, NSW: St Paul's Publications, 2005), 13.

28. Armitage, *A Twofold Solidarity*, 17.

29. Joseph Torrell, "Présentation," in Jean-Pierre Torrell, O. P., *Le Christ en ses Mystères: La vie et l'oeuvre de Jésus selon saint Thomas d'Aquin* (Paris: Desclée, 1999), I. 4. Emphasis in the original.

30. Ibid., 21. Thomists are not agreed on the question of how Christ's saving acts in his historical existence reach the redeemed with gracious effect. Torrell prefers to the opinion that the instrumental cause of grace is Christ's glorified humanity "inasmuch as it is 'modified' by the mysteries of that earthly life," the view that "[i]nasmuch as it operates *in virtute divina*, the act posed by Christ is not subject to time, for God has the privilege in his eternity of touching beings which are for us past or future, as if they were present," Jean-Pierre Torrell, *Saint Thomas Aquinas. Volume 2, Spiritual Master*, 135, 138.

Chapter Three

God

In and through all of the above, the God the Holy Trinity entered history. The word "history," when taken in conjunction with the word "Trinity," draws attention to the self-involvement in history of the God who is, in different senses, both One and Three. This makes imperative some comment on the theology of God. For the moment, I leave to one side the question of the "trinity" of God. For now I focus rather on the conjunction of the words "God" and "history." How can the Eternal and time be conjoined in a phrase, and the truth of such conjoining made credible?

We live in a world of finitude, a world characterized by limits—and indeed in a world of finitudes, a world composed of finite entities. And yet, as the German Lutheran theologian Wolfhart Pannenberg noted, the very idea of a finite reality would appear to presuppose or to "posit" (as philosophers say) the idea of infinity. That is, any act of distinguishing one reality in its limitedness from another such reality presupposes what Pannenberg calls an "encompassing field within which all those differences occur."[1] The French rationalist philosopher René Descartes, in the third of his celebrated *Meditations*, had asserted for this reason the "priority" of the infinite vis-à-vis the finite. And he had in mind that priority not just as it occurs in our thinking about reality but as it holds good in reality itself. In this matter, Descartes was following a long line of Christian metaphysicians going back at least to St. Gregory of Nyssa in the fourth century. For St. Gregory, thinking (as he was) over against the pagan metaphysics of the Hellenic philosophers, the nature of God is infinite, and this being-beyond-everything-finite is why Scripture can conceive of the "radical otherness" of a God who is "not bound to any place 'up there' or 'out there,' but can also be fully present within the world of finite realities."[2] The Swiss dogmatician Hans

Urs von Balthasar, explains, drawing into the account as he does so that latest
of all late medieval theologians, Nicholas of Cusa:

> Here we must be mindful of the fact that God, as absolute being as opposed to
> all finite existents, is indeed the "Wholly Other"; but, precisely for this reason,
> he is also the "Not Other" (*Non-Aliud*), as Nicholas of Cusa says. God is able,
> therefore, to reveal in Christ at once God and man, and this not in alternation,
> as is often suggested simplistically, but simultaneously. Yet this occurs in such
> a way that the relativity of the human (as creaturely) does not appear to be
> oppressed and violated by the simultaneous absoluteness of the divine.[3]

With this truth in hand, the further question of God as Trinity can be
broached as well. The Incarnation in the humanity of Jesus Christ of the
Word who is consubstantial with the Father and the Holy Spirit, should be
considered the supreme vindication of the openness of Infinity to otherness
Balthasar has just been speaking about. A Unity that is not the bare oneness
of a Monad but the fulness of reciprocal relations knows the "Other" within
itself as the ground of possibility of "another" beyond itself. There is in the
Trinity a Source (the Father), an Expression (the Son or Word), and a Spirit
(the Holy Spirit) that at once unites the Source and its Expression and guar-
antees the difference between them—without which they would be reducible
to that "bare" monadic One to which the unity that is "fulness of reciprocal
relations" can only be alien and make no sense. And furthermore, owing to
the "non-other" character of divine Infinity, the Father and the Spirit can
render the Word a member of God's own creation—"Another" in a further
sense, when the Word takes to himself an example of human creaturehood
without that Word ceasing to be God. The expressiveness of the Son (he *is*
the Father's Expression) can inhere not only in eternal being in God but in
temporal being in the world.

Once "made man," the Word incarnate used the humanity he had "assumed" (i.e., taken to himself) to communicate to the world a share in the
essential quality of divine life. This he did—communicating the graciousness
of God—in the action-events of his human story. That is the reason for the
Christian's habitual return to those events, year after year with the Liturgy,
and day after day in personal meditation. Through what the Latin Scholastics
would call "exemplar causality," those key events in the life of Jesus Christ,
events at once historical (their acting or acted-upon subject is a human being)
and meta-historical (this same agent is also personally divine), can mark
other human lives with their own essential form. In the ancient technology of
authentication, seals sink deep into wax the outline they carry.

Here of course Scripture comes first since it is through the biblically
attested history that divine revelation takes place in time. Unless the principal
events in the life of Jesus Christ genuinely happened (and for this the historical reliability of the Gospels is indispensable), the question of their continu-

ing provision of resources for the relation between God and ourselves does not arise. By way of assistance in coming to terms with the Scripturally attested "happenings," I shall be studying these key events with help from exegetes who think with the mind of the Great Church (these may be Catholic, Orthodox or Anglican), and through the eyes of the Fathers and the anonymous composers of the liturgical sources, as well as St. Thomas, his late-nineteenth-century disciple Abbot Columba Marmion, and two twentieth-century theologians, Hans Urs von Balthasar, and the Orthodox theologian who most resembles him, Sergius Bulgakov. This selection of sources and aids corresponds to those that feature in my programmatic statement *Chalice of God.*[4] As in that work, I shall also draw on the illustrative power of iconography, albeit evoked in words, not visual reproductions.

In every key event in the life of Christ, God was at work in his Son to shape minds, hearts, and imaginations, so that human beings can draw forever after on these inexhaustible sources. This is why it is correct to speak, with Marmion, and with, indeed, the premier Dominican study of Aquinas on the same topic, of "Christ in his mysteries." [5] These mystery-events are not just historical occurrences that, like all such events, belong to the human past. Because their acting subject was not simply a man but the God-man, they have that further meta-historical dimension. They are permanently able to affect the intended beneficiary of the mysteries: namely, the human race. In Marmion's words,

> It is true that in their historical, material duration the mysteries of Christ's life on earth are now past; but their power remains, and the grace that allows us to share in them operates always. . . . Threefold reason why the mysteries of Jesus are ours: Christ lived them for us; in them Jesus reveals Himself as our Exemplar; and in them He unites us with Himself.[6]

The Fathers, the Liturgies, Thomas, Marmion, Balthasar, Bulgakov, all furnish in different ways a Trinitarian reading of the key events of the Christological narrative, which itself is the record of the "deep mysteries."

Thomas's account of the "action-events" in which the grace of Christ was poured out in history by the Father's incarnate Son gave us an initial glimpse of how "history" and "the Trinity" are conjoined in this subject matter. Only Incarnation makes full sense of the gospel witnesses, yes. But only Trinity makes full sense of Incarnation. In the words of the English New Testament scholar N. T. Wright,

> From the very earliest Christian documents we possess (i.e., the letters of Paul) right through mainstream Christianity to the fifth century and beyond, we find Christians straining every nerve to say what they found themselves compelled to say: *not* that there were now two, or three, different Gods but that the one true God had revealed himself to be, within himself so to speak, irrevocably

threefold. The whole point of the doctrine of the Trinity, both in its early
stages in passages like Galatians 4:1–7, 1 Corinthians 12:4–6, 2 Corinthians
13:13, and Matthew 28:19, and in its later stages in the writings of the Greek
and Latin Fathers, was that one could not say that there was a plurality of
Gods; only that there was an irreducible threefold-ness about the one God. [7]

How, then, is the Trinity revealed in the New Testament, which of course
for the "Great Church" the Trinity definitely is—so much is presumed by the
Creeds and the historic Liturgies—even if scholars of early Christianity,
including some with ecclesial connections, have sometimes sought to revise
downward the findings of the patristic age, whether through Binitarianism,
suppressing the divinity of the Son or the Spirit, or Unitarianism, suppressing
the divinity of them both.

The answer commonly presumed by exegetes is that the Trinitarianism of
the New Testament finds its expression in the teaching offered by the "speak-
ers" in the texts: preeminently, by Jesus himself, notably in the Gospel according to John, but not excluding apostolic voices in the Letters, especially
those of Paul.

Yet dogmatic theology has frequently sought to take a different—a complementary rather than alternative—tack, by locating Trinitarianism in the
events described in the Gospels. Here the great theophany scenes of the
Baptism of Christ and his Transfiguration spring first to mind. This is so
despite whether dogmatic theologians think of the revelation of the triune
God in certain key events in the Gospel narrative as supplementary to the
teaching already mentioned (and hence secondary), or whether, rather, they
consider those events to be the primordial foundation on which the teaching
rests (and hence primary). The word "complementary" can cover both those
approaches. And certainly we need a coherent account of how the Trinity
may be said to be disclosed in crucial events in the life of Christ, including
there his Death and Resurrection—which Resurrection, after all, is itself a
mode of new life. [8] In Balthasar's words, "Although the Son alone becomes
man, not the Father or the Spirit, the Son's human life necessarily *exhibits
aspects* of his relationship to the Father and to the Spirit." [9]

It is instructive to compare the cases of Aquinas and Balthasar in this
regard. In the case of St. Thomas, though he has a marked interest in how the
divine Persons are active in distinct yet essentially related ways in various
events in the life of Christ (these range from his Conception to his Ascension
and "Session"), he is at least equally preoccupied with the question of how
the divine nature and power are expressed through the humanity of Jesus.
This latter emphasis on the manifestation of the Uncreated via the created
tends to elide somewhat his concern for the unique role of the different
Trinitarian Persons. That is more the case because Thomas holds to the
principle that "the works of the Trinity are common"—even if that principle

cannot, of course, abolish the quite evidently special self-involvement of the Son, the second divine Person, in his own Incarnation and in the events that follow from it. Thomas does what he can to expand the space for a Trinitarianism of events by stressing the way the eternal hypostatic particularities of this or that divine Person (deriving from their mode of procession, for the Spirit and the Son, or lack of such a mode, for the Father) indicate congruencies with this or that divine action in the Gospel story.

As to Hans Urs von Balthasar, here the position is almost the reverse of Thomas's, even if both "masters" have it in common that they seek to offer to the reader a sustained account of the mysteries of the life of Christ within a Trinitarian doctrine of God. In the case of Balthasar, interest in the general relation of the Godhead to the humanity of Christ, in what the latter did and underwent, takes a back seat. Balthasar is little concerned with the duality of natures of the second Person in his incarnate life (to the point that, if we did not know better, this could look like Monophysitism). Instead, he is very much preoccupied with the distinctive agency of the Three (to the extent that, were we not alerted to other affirmations in his corpus of writing, this could appear to approximate to Tritheism). Balthasar presents the key Gospel moments as "relational" events whereby the interplay of the Persons receives ever fuller determination.

It is less easy to find here, at first sight, the unity of God. But Balthasar's understanding of the generation of the Son shows that the unity of the action of the Trinitarian persons in the divine essence is infinitely greater than the unity of the action of a human person. For Balthasar accepts Aquinas's view that the generation (the "procession") of the Son is one single act of Father and Son in which the *potentia generari* (the "power to be generated") of the Son corresponds to the *potentia generandi* (the "power of generating") of the Father, a view shared by Thomas's great Franciscan contemporary St. Bonaventure,[10] on whose commentary on the *Book of the Sentences*—the standard early medieval textbook in theology—Balthasar explicitly draws.[11] This insight is of fundamental importance, especially (so we shall see) for an adequate understanding of the Cross as a Trinitarian act.[12] What happened on the Cross, presented initially as the abandonment of the Son by the Father, can only be properly viewed in the light of the Resurrection—where it turns out that Father and Son were never more united in the Spirit than they were in the Paschal Mystery.

The single operation, stressed by Thomas, need not entail the indistinctness of the Persons, avoided by Balthasar, in that very acting. In the well-devised formula of the Franco-Hungarian scholar Etienne Vetö (whose account of Thomas and Balthasar I have been following here), the mysteries of the life of Christ exhibit "one operation in three activities."[13]

To make full sense of the life, death, and Resurrection of Christ *and how they affect ourselves*, such a full-bloodedly Trinitarian perspective is definitely required. As supplied here, I make two basic claims. First, the world is aboriginally related to the Son and thus to the entire divine Trinity. By virtue of my existence as a creature, I am already in a relation of a kind to the One who became man as Jesus Christ, the Trinitarian Son. Secondly, Father, Son and Spirit are, by their relations of origin and of communion, in a primordial condition of mutual surrender, in an eternal sacrifice of which the Son's sacrifice on earth (and its acceptance in Heaven) is the outworking—the outworking in a world which, though made through him, has fallen into corruption. This means that the message of Jesus—sacrificial love—is also the message of the eternal God and ever has been.

These theses are characteristically Balthasarian but they are not exclusive to him. The first thesis can be paralleled in much of the classic theology of the Latin Church, for example, in the Prologue to St. Thomas's *Writing on the Sentences*. In creation, the Son, who is the divine Wisdom, has "caused streams to flow from him."[14] The second has been adopted, at least in part, from the Russian Orthodox theological tradition, and notably from its greatest systematic thinker, Sergius Bulgakov.

First, then, on Christ and creation, *the world is aboriginally related to the Son and thus to the entire divine Trinity*. The Son as the Father's Word and Expression is, in the language of the High Scholastics, the "efficient cause" of creation, the One *through* whom all things were made. He is also the "final cause" of creation—the One *for* whom all things were made. But in addition—and here is the peculiar emphasis of Balthasar—the Son is the "exemplar cause" of creation, the One *in* whom all things are made, in such a way that all things can be eloquent, expressive. That is certainly not alien to the thought of the Fathers: in his *On Eighty-Three Different Questions*, Augustine wrote, "[T]he Son is the first species by which, so to speak, all things are specified, and the form by which all things are formed."[15] And as to Thomas, in his commentary on the Letter to the Colossians, we read, "The Platonists posited Ideas, saying that whatsoever thing comes to be does so by participating in an Idea. Instead of these [many] ideas we have one reality, namely, the Son, the Word of God."[16] But Balthasar insists on the further possibilities this understanding opens up. The world, and in a special way the rational creation whose powers of knowledge and love render the creation more fully like the Logos, shares, however modestly, in the Son's role as Expression— his role as Expression vis-à-vis the ultimate Source, the Father. Things are always, by virtue of creation, "in" the Son and therefore they are capable, in however limited a way, of expressing the Son's relation with the Father. In the prologue to his commentary on a more ancient text, the *On the Trinity* of the sixth century Latin Christian philosopher Boethius, Thomas approaches this position when he finds in the Son's birth from the Father the "foundation of every birth out of what is other than itself."[17] The eminent Thomist commentator Jean-Pierre Torrell wrote,

From the point of view of nature, the perfection of creatures represents the perfection of the divine nature only very imperfectly. This is quite clear, but we must nonetheless trace their perfection back to its explanatory principle in the Son, who contains all the perfection of the divine nature, since he is the perfect image of the Father. In this way, the procession of the Son is the model, the exemplar, and the reason for the procession of creatures in the natural order, where they imitate and reproduce something of the divine nature.[18]

Does such a world, we may ask, "add" anything to God? It can be said to do so only in the sense that it is a further expression of the Father/Son relation, and hence of the eternal Trinitarian "event" of Father, Son, and Holy Spirit whereby God is God.[19] In the words of a Jesuit expounder of Balthasar's thought, "This means that the existence of God and the world together is not greater than the existence of God alone, except in the sense that God himself as Trinitarian event of love is 'always-greater.'"[20]

What then of the second key Trinitarian notion invoked in the account of the mysteries of Christ that will follow here, the claim that *the Trinity is eternal self-surrender*? There is a connection between the two claims, as Balthasar makes plain. If the very ideas of things, their inmost structure and identity, are "in" the Word, then they are "grounded in the Father, which implies not only the power of self-expression but also the power of self-surrender—just as, in Trinitarian terms, the Son, in receiving himself from the Father, also receives the (natural) will to breathe forth the Spirit, to attune himself to that self-surrender which characterizes generation by the Father."[21]

The New Testament revelation, as Jesus, of the Father's Son—*the* Revealer—shows the profound linkage that exists between glory and such self-surrender (or "self-emptying"). In the exegete Richard Bauckham's words, "The exaltation of Christ to participation in the unique divine sovereignty shows him to be included in the unique divine identity. But since the exalted Christ is first the humiliated Christ, since indeed it is *because* of his self-abnegation that he is exalted, his humiliation belongs to the identity of God as truly as his exaltation does. The identity of God—who God is—is revealed as much in self-abasement and service as it is in exaltation and rule. The God who is high can also be low, because God is God not in seeking his own advantage but in self-giving. His self-giving in abasement and service ensures that his sovereignty over all things is also a form of his self-giving."[22]

And again, "Because God is who God is in his gracious self-giving, God's identity appears in the loving service and self-abnegation to death of his Son. Because God is who God is in his gracious self-giving, God's identity, we can say, is not simply revealed but enacted in the event of salvation for the world which the service and self-humiliation of his Son accomplishes."[23] It is an extraordinary fulfillment of Isaiah 57:15—"Thus says the exalted and lofty One who inhabits eternity, whose name is Holy: 'I dwell in the high and lowly place, and also with those who are crushed and lowly in spirit,'" a fulfillment of that Old Testament text in which God dwells not only *with* the lowly but *as* the Lowly.

What Bauckham does not speak of is the retrojection of this feature of divine identity to its source—in the self-giving (*to each other*, this can only be) of the Trinitarian Persons.[24] Here is where Hans Urs von Balthasar and his Russian forerunner Sergius Bulgakov can better serve our turn. For all orthodox theology, the affirmation of St. John in his First Letter that "God is love" (I John 4:8) is understood not just intransitively but transitively. As the divine Trinity, God is an exchange of love, the Father giving himself to the Son who reciprocates that gift by and in the Holy Spirit. Echoing the mystic with whom he associated so much in his theology, Adrienne von Speyr, Balthasar speaks of the "surrendered Son . . . the surrendering Father and . . . the Spirit, who is himself this surrender."[25] For Balthasar, our ability to speak of divine self-giving in such terms turns on the applicability to the Trinitarian Persons of the language of *passivity and renunciation*—shorn, however, of the negative connotations these concepts bring with them when employed to speak of created persons (or, where "passivity" is concerned, of things). For the concepts of passivity and renunciation seem prerequisite if the notion of self-surrender is to enjoy full value. Without a "receptive let-ting-be," indeed, all "giving" is a problematic process.[26]

This will have repercussions for the self-involvement of the triune God, through Jesus Christ, in the story of the world, and not least in the mystery of his Passion. The Jesuit theologian Jean Galot wrote of the divine Persons, who from all eternity "bring forth one another through "reciprocal surrender of self":

> The ecstasy is not painful in itself, it is the pure power of love. But the innermost self-renunciation it implies—an aspect of the ardour of self-surren-der—can be seen as the primal origin of renunciations bound up with love for humankind, and these have their painful side.[27]

But if Balthasar's Christian metaphysic is to stay aligned, as he claims it is, with the fundamental metaphysics of St. Thomas, then the ideas of passiv-ity (or receptivity) and renunciation (or letting-be) will need to be compatible with the absolutely basic and non-negotiable affirmation of Thomist ontolo-gy that God is *Actus Purus*: "sheer actuality," "pure act"—with nothing merely "potential" about it. They must be understood, that is to say, not as deficiencies but, on the contrary, as *positive perfections*.

> [W]ithin the Trinity the positive nature of receptivity or passivity is seen by the way in which the Son receives his being from the Father, the Holy Spirit from Father and Son, without any suggestion that this receptivity betrays a

lack of being as in the case with potency in the realm of creation whose origins are *ex nihilo*. Similarly in the Father, while there is of course no loss of his divinity, there is in the "generation" of the Son a surrendering . . . of being God on his own, a certain renunciation and then communication of all that he is and has. One stammers in the attempt to speak of these mysterious passivities— already referred to also as modalities—within the divine *actus purus*.[28]

That quite legitimate caveat now entered, we can prudently approach the idea of Trinitarian self-surrender or *Urkenosis,* this time as expressed by Bulgakov. It is crucial to his "Great Trilogy"—*The Lamb of God, The Comforter,* and *The Bride of the Lamb*. But it is also found, and more accessibly, in his sermon collection *Tserkovnaia Radost'*: "Churchly Joy."

God is he who in the Trinity renounces Himself from all eternity in the reciprocal love of the Three Hypostases; for "God is love," and "the unfathomable divine power of the holy and glorious Cross" is the power of God's life—of all-conquering, immeasurable love *in the depths* of the Holy Trinity itself.[29]

The creation of the world, by giving place to being that is not God himself, is already an act of self-renunciation. But it is exceeded in the redemptive actions whereby God brought back to himself a world that, alienated from him by sin, was falling into disintegration and despair. Not only does the Father yield up his Only Begotten Son, the Spirit "agrees to descend into the fallen and embittered world, where He reposes upon Christ the Anointed and makes His abode in Christ's Mother, thus fulfilling the Church."[30] Such is the threefold sacrifice, Paternal, Filial, and "Spiritual," of the one and indivisible Trinity.

So the Passion begins with the Birth. "The Cave is the sepulcher in the vineyard; the infant's linens are the winding sheets."[31] In the words of an American scholar concerned to show the commonality between Bulgakov and Balthasar, this "mode of perfect, absolute, self-sacrificial, and ecstatic love, which is constitutive for divine personhood, is that which substantially and essentially is divinity. To sound a Johannine theme, God *is* Love."[32] Or in Balthasar's own words, "Only when truth is seen to have a Trinitarian form does the assertion that God is love—burning, consuming, judging and redeeming love—become evident for the world as a whole. And truth can only be seen to be Trinitarian when One of the Trinity becomes man and, in human form, interprets eternal Love to us."[33] And here, in the life of Jesus, "All the contingent 'abasements' of God in the economy of salvation are forever included and outstripped in the eternal event of Love."[34]

The linking of the initial and final abasements in the Christ-narrative, as laid out so strikingly in the Russian sermons by Bulgakov just quoted, is not something unknown to the Latin Church. Those who have attended the Roman Liturgy for Passiontide will no doubt have sung the great hymn by

Venantius Fortunatus, which also joins together Easter and Christmas in a *prima facie* disconcerting way. The hymn writer fuses Mary's wrapping the Bethlehem Babe in "linen bands" with the Golgotha mourners' wrapping of the Savior's dead body in a winding sheet. It is Bulgakov who gives us the key to the Latin hymn by showing how Christmas and Easter form a single sacrificial movement the origin of which must be sought in the Holy Trinity itself. Iconographically, Bulgakov enables one to see the point of those Western images of the Crib of Christ ,which depict it as a coffin, for here Christmas and Good Friday are one.

For the origination of both mysteries (Birth and life-giving Death) in God the Holy Trinity, another Western image is pertinent. It is the "Throne of Grace." In that image the incarnate and crucified Christ is lovingly held by the Father, with the Dove of the Holy Spirit occupying the space between. It suggests a Trinitarian confession of the kind made by the Byzantine Liturgy. We confess God the Father, Creator of the world visible and invisible, doing all things through the Son with the participation of the Holy Spirit. We confess God the Son, the Redeemer, through whom we have known the Father and through whom the Holy Spirit came into the world. And we confess God the Holy Spirit, the Comforter, proceeding from the Father and resting in the Son, giving life to all things.

At Pentecost, the divine creative and saving activity—which bears with it the identity of its Agents, Father, Son, and Spirit—came to its culmination for man's sanctification, as the final fulfillment of the promises to Israel, closing the cycle of the mysteries but also opening them out to human access for evermore—an "evermore" itself finalized in the Parousia of the Lord. The Trinitarian self-involvement must be borne in mind in any account of the mysteries of Christ.

NOTES

1. Wolfhart Pannenberg, *An Introduction to Systematic Theology* (Grand Rapids, MI: Eerdmans, 1991), 30.

2. Pannenberg, *An Introduction to Systematic Theology.*

3. Hans Urs von Balthasar, *The Glory of the Lord: A Theological Aesthetics, I: Seeing the Form,* 459.

4. Aidan Nichols, O. P., *Chalice of God. A Systematic Theology in Outline* (Collegeville, MN, Liturgical Press, 2012).

5. Columba Marmion, *Christ in His Mysteries* (Bethesda, MD: Zacchaeus Press, 2008); Jean-Pierre Torrell, *Le Christ en ses Mystères,* op. cit., passim.

6. Columba Marmion, *Christ in His Mysteries,* 20, 12.

7. N. T. Wright, *Who Was Jesus?* (London: SPCK, 1992), 53.

8. Etienne Vetö, *Du Christ à la Trinité: Penser les Mystères du Christ après Thomas d'Aquin et Balthasar* (Paris: Editions du Cerf, 2012).

9. Hans Urs von Balthasar, *Prayer* (San Francisco, CA: Ignatius, 1986), 184.

10. Hans Urs von Balthasar, *Theo-Drama: Theological Dramatic Theory, V: The Last Act* (San Francisco, CA: Ignatius, 1998), 85–88.

11. Hans Urs von Balthasar, *Theo-Drama*, 85.

12. See Martin Bieler, "God and the Cross. The Doctrine of God in the Work of Hans Urs von Balthasar," *Communio* 42 (2015), 61–88, and here at 68–69.

13. Etienne Vetö, *Du Christ à la Trinité: Penser les Mystères du Christ après Thomas d'Aquin et Balthasar*, 425–47.

14. Thomas Aquinas, *Writing on the Sentences,* I., prologue.

15. Augustine, *Eighty-Three Different Questions* (Washington, DC: Catholic University of America Press, 1982), 50.

16. Thomas Aquinas, *Commentary on Colossians*, chapter 1, I. 4; cf. Thomas Aquinas, *Summa theologiae* Ia, q, 46, a. 3. This should not of course be taken as excluding a role for the Holy Spirit in creation, since the Father creates through his Love (the Spirit) as well as his Word (the Son), as is emphasised in Aquinas, Ia., q. 45, a. 6.

17. Thomas Aquinas, *Commentary on Boethius on the Trinity*, prologue. On the procession of persons as the ratio of both creation and creation's return in Christ to God, see Gilles Emery, O. P., *La Trinité créatrice: Trinité et Création dans les commentaries aux Sentences de Thomas d'Aquin et de ses précurseurs Albert le Grand et Bonaventure* (Paris: Vrin, 1994), and the summary thereof in Gilles Emery, O. P., "Trinité et creation: Le principe trinitaire de la création dans les Commentaires d'Albert le Grand, de Bonaventure et de Thomas d'Aquin sur less Sentences," *Revue des sciences philosophiques et théologiques* 79 (1995), 405–30.

18. Jean-Pierre Torrell, O. P., *Saint Thomas Aquinas: Volume 2, Spiritual Master*, 59, with reference to Thomas's *Writing on the Sentences*, I., dist. 14, q. 2, a. 2. Thomas makes a corresponding claim for the role of the Holy Spirit in the origination and return of the world, based on the liberality of God expressed in the spiration of the Spirit who is Love.

19. Gerard O'Hanlon, S. J., *The Immutability of God in the Theology of Hans Urs von Balthasar* (Cambridge: Cambridge University Press, 1990), 51.

20. O'Hanlon, S. J., *The Immutability of God in the Theology of Hans Urs von Balthasar*, 55.

21. Hans Urs von Balthasar, *Theo-Drama: Theological Dramatic Theory, V: The Last Act*, 75.

22. Richard Bauckham, *God Crucified: Monotheism and Christology in the New Testament* (Carlisle: Paternoster, 1998), 61.

23. Bauckham, *God Crucified*, 68.

24. He does, however, concede that "[n]othing in the Second Temple Jewish understanding of divine identity contradicts the possibility of inter-personal relationship within the divine Identity," while adding "but on the other hand there is little, if anything, that anticipates it," Bauckham, *God Crucified*, 75.

25. Hans Urs von Balthasar, *Theo-Drama: Theological Dramatic Theory, V: The Last Act*, 121.

26. Hans Urs von Balthasar, *Theo-Drama*, 86.

27. Jean Galot, S. J., *Dieu, souffre-t-il?* (Paris: Lethellieux, 1976), 175–76.

28. Gerard O'Hanlon, S. J., *The Immutability of God in the Theology of Hans Urs von Balthasar*, 67. Balthasar's decision to speak of not only love but also hope and faith (and worship) as suitable terms to describe the communion in surrender of the Persons exemplifies what in *Chalice of God* I called "rhetorical excesses" in his work (here, as so often in such moments, he is citing Adrienne von Speyr). There must be a limit to anthropomorphism, even an anthropomorphism based on the fundamental attitudes of graced personality. He would doubtless reply that some place must be found for these "excesses" if the "trinitarian conversation is the prototype of all prayer": Hans Urs von Balthasar, *Theo-Drama: Theological Dramatic Theory, V: The Last Act*, 96.

29. Sergius Bulgakov, *Churchly Joy: Orthodox Devotions for the Church Year* (Grand Rapids, MI: Eerdmans, 2008), 89.

30. Bulgakov, *Churchly Joy*, 4.

31. Bulgakov, *Churchly Joy*, 28.

32. Jennifer Newsome Martin, *Hans Urs von Balthasar and the Critical Appropriation of Russian Religious Thought* (Notre Dame, IN: University of Notre Dame Press, 2015), 190.

33. Hans Urs von Balthasar, *Prayer*, 182.

34. Hans Urs von Balthasar, *Mysterium Paschale: The Mystery of Easter* (Edinburgh: T. and T. Clark, 1990), ix.

Chapter Four

The Mysteries and Ourselves

Here I wish to go through the principal Christological mysteries, *for them-selves* and *in ourselves*. Doubtless their number could be differently assessed, whether as rather more or somewhat less. I am taking them to be the Annunciation, the Nativity, the Baptism, the Transfiguration, the Passion and Death, the Descent into Hell, the Resurrection, the Ascension, Pentecost, and the Second Coming. In the language of Leo the Great, deciding how many mysteries to number is equivalent to determining which events in the life of Christ should count as constituting the *sacramentum salutis*, the "sacrament of salvation,"[1] or, in another formulation, the "principal works of Christ whose totality constitutes the *opus salutis*," "the work of salvation."[2]

For each mystery I offer some remarks, first on the biblical material; then on the mystery as seen by the Liturgy and the Fathers; then again as discussed by the great theological masters mentioned in the previous chapter, and finally I look at one or more examples of its reflection in the art of the Church. (Owing to the *embarras de richesse*, these will largely be from the Byzantine-Slav tradition, though in the case of the Passion and Death I cast my net more widely.) From these sources, the significance of each mystery for ourselves may be ascertained. The mystery is not only commemorated. It is celebrated, which means in this context three things. It is gratefully received; it is formative for us, and in it God in Christ is accessed. In this way the mystery that was Christ's becomes our own. To recall Marmion's succinct summary already cited, "Threefold reason why the mysteries of Jesus are ours: Christ lived them for us; in them Jesus reveals Himself as our Exemplar; and in them He unites us with Himself."[3]

It is not inappropriate here to cite an excellent passage of *Sacrosanctum Concilium*, the Constitution on the Liturgy of the Second Vatican Council, which has this to say of the worshipping Church, mediatrix of the relation of the Trinity-in-Christ to those who are in time. "In the course of the year, she unfolds the whole mystery of Christ from the incarnation and nativity to the ascension, to Pentecost and the expectation of the blessed hope of the coming of the Lord. Thus recalling the mysteries of the redemption, she opens up to the faithful the riches of her Lord's powers and merits, so that these are in some way made present for all time; the faithful lay hold of them and are filled with saving grace."[4] That passage relies heavily on what Pope Pius XII had to say about the efficacy of the mysteries of Christ as presented by the liturgical year in his 1947 encyclical on the Sacred Liturgy, *Mediator Dei*.

On the efficacy of those mysteries, Dom Marie Bernard de Soos, special-ist in the liturgical theology of St. Leo, writing in the year before Pius's death, had this to say: "The Pope, by qualifying them as *fontes divinae gratiae*, ascribed to them in effect an importance the theologian can compare to that of the sacraments."[5] Only a study which synthesized a wide variety of relevant materials, de Soos went on, could do the matter justice. What is presented in the chapters that follow hardly constitutes the adequate account de Soos desired. But at least it represents, in a miniature fashion, the aim of a "synthesis" on whose importance he insisted.[6] The preface to this book, appealing to the metaphor of a "cocktail," already suggested, in perhaps too frivolous a fashion, how this is so.

The mysteries cannot have the effect that is claimed for them unless their relation to time is unique. The Liturgy that celebrates them belongs not only to cosmic time (the time of nature), or to historical time (the time of man), but to the time of salvation as well. "This last and mysterious reference, which claims to be neither a simple memory nor a future event, goes beyond the possibilities of the present. It supposes that Christ is "now," at the mo-ment when the Liturgy unfolds, seated at the right hand of God, and thus the time of the Liturgy encounters in a certain manner God's *eternity*."[7] It fol-lows that the time of the saving events cannot be, despite their authentically historical character, an "enclosed" time; it must be a time that opens out through divine action onto other times too. God's *durée* is not like ours; it knows no succession as our time does. The event whose subject is Christ is indeed a "once for all" event, but it is so in a sense that "no human fact verifies" for it is a mystery.[8] It is, moreover, a mystery that finds an answer-ing mystery in that of the Church. "If the time of the Church is also deeply qualified by its past and its future it must be the case that the reality acquired by that past and promised for that future is contemporary with her—in fact, the same Christ who is risen and will come again reigns sitting at God's right."[9]

NOTES

1. Marie Bernard de Soos, *Le Mystere liturgique d'après saint Léon le Grand* (Münster: Aschendorff, 1958), 38.

2. De Soos, *Le Mystere liturgique*, 52.

3. Columba Marmion, *Christ in His Mysteries* (Bethesda, MD: Zacchaeus Press, 2008), 12.

4. *Sacrosanctum Concilium*, 102.

5. Marie Bernard de Soos, *Le Mystere liturgique d'après saint Léon le Grand*, 2.

6. De Soos, *Le Mystere liturgique*.

7. Thomas G. Chifflot, O. P., "Le Christ et le temps," *La Maison-Dieu* 13 (1948), 26–49, and here at 26. Emphasis in the original. Chiflot had his sights on Oscar Cullmann's study *Christus und die Zeit: Die urchristliche Zeit- and Geschichtsauffassung* (Zurich: Evangelischer Verlag, 1946).

8. Thomas G. Chifflot, O. P., "Le Christ et le temps," art. cit., 45.

9. Chifflot, "Le Christ et le temps, 47.

Chapter Five

Annunciation

The evangelist Matthew locates an Annunciation to Joseph as the climax of a genealogy of Jesus that starts with Abraham. For an Annunciation to Mary, the evangelist Luke offers a genealogy going back to Adam, the ultimate human beginning. Though, evidently, these genealogies differ, and do so for good reasons,[1] they both end in a virginal Conception and a Birth. It needs no explanation that those who had accepted the claims of Jesus—or, in the case of St. Luke's correspondent Theophilus, had begun to accept those claims—should be interested in his origins. A total absence of such interest would surely be odd. So the Gospel books of Matthew and Luke, in starting with human beginnings, do not omit to speak of the ancestry of the Lord.

St. Matthew's Gospel gives a legal succession list for Joseph that makes Jesus a lawful heir to the throne of David. At the same time, the "designation of Jesus as 'son of Abraham' suggests that he is that 'seed' of Abraham by whom 'all the nations of the earth shall bless themselves'" (Genesis 22:18).[2] For the Hebrew Bible, there is an important connection between Abraham and David. The Davidic dynasty was to be the means whereby the promises to Abraham of a world-wide significance would be attained. That is the proper sense of "Messiahship." A Gospel book designed to show that Jesus is Israel's Messiah could not have dispensed with a genealogy of approximately this kind.

By contrast, St. Luke's Gospel gives a selection from Joseph's family tree. Or on another theory, it is Mary's ancestry that Luke gives. At any rate, in the patristic age it will be assumed that Mary is a Davidide, just like her husband. Indeed, the village of Mary, Nazareth, which seemingly took its name from the "branch," *netser*, "of Jesse," is thought to have been a historic center of lateral descendants of King David.[3]

St. Matthew's convenient arrangement of three-times-fourteen genera-
tions has a symmetry designed to suggest how Jesus's descent and Conception is providential. That symmetry is only possible through deliberate omis-
sions in the evangelist's sources—perhaps on the rabbinic principle that
grandchildren can be regarded as children. The number "fourteen" may derive from the practice called *gematria*: in Hebrew or Greek script, numbers
are really letters and so are convertible into names, and, as it happens, *fourteen* is the numerical value of David's name in its Hebrew spelling.[4] So this
would be another way of saying, the One to be born is David's son. What
about the "three" in "three-times-fourteen"? Matthew may have in mind
three half-portions of a lunar month: the first, when the moon is waxing, to
end in David; the second, when it is waning, to end in the Exile and the
apparent failure of the promise; and the third, when it is waxing again, to
climax in Jesus, who is David's heir. In the Lucan genealogy come many
more names—seventy-seven in all, perhaps to be understood as eleven-
times-seven. That would suggest the Jewish way of reckoning world history
as consisting in twelve (eleven-plus-one) epochs. In that case, Jesus would
initiate the twelfth—and concluding—age of the world.[5] The theme of eschatology—vital to the mysteries, for they are in time yet time-transcending—is
already in play.

The unique circumstances of the Annunciation event are prefigured in the
Matthaean genealogy. In the women named in Matthew's list—up to but
excluding Mary—divine action had served to "overcome the moral or biolog-
ical irregularity of the human parents."[6] But now, in Mary of Nazareth, that
action goes further. Here it "overcomes the total absence of the father's
begetting."[7] Once again, the message runs: history is coming to a climax, it is
entering on its final, "eschatological," phase. When this Gospel book draws
to its close, we shall hear the risen Christ declare, "Behold I am with you all
days, even until the end of the world" (Matthew 28:20). These words renew
the eschatological motif once sounded as the Gospel began.

As already mentioned, St. Matthew's account of the Lord's conception is
written from the standpoint of Joseph, rather than Mary. The Dominican
exegete Marie-Joseph Lagrange explains why: "Matthew abstracts from the
annunciation of the angel Gabriel to Mary because he is only concerned with
Jesus' legal situation in relation to Joseph who will have to accept the official
paternity."[8] But in the Annunciation of a birth where the mother is a virgin
and the "father" is God himself—acting by direct divine power to make his
own Word the personal subject of the human embryo—St. Joseph's role can
only be one of self-effacement. Appropriately enough, then, the news is
communicated to him by way of dream. A dream can involve cognition—
learning things. But it can hardly involve consent—the positive acceptance
of a task. It is the latter that was asked of Mary, and her consent is therefore
the master theme of St. Luke's version of the Annunciation mystery.

Despite Luke's comparative lack of interest in Joseph, he sings from the same hymn-sheet as Matthew on the virginal Conception. That Conception had belonged to Messianic prophecy ever since the Septuagint translators opted to render Isaiah's Hebrew term "young woman," *almah*, by the Greek word *parthenos*. The Septuagint is the source of almost all the Old Testament citations in the New Testament. And it predominates in the monuments of Tradition: the writings of the Fathers and the texts of the liturgies. The Old Latin Bible, in its variant forms, was essentially translated from the Septuagint. The Septuagint remains strongly present in St. Jerome's Vulgate version—despite his appeal to "Hebrew truth." Though Jewish in origin, the Septuagint Bible has thus become "Christian Scripture."[9]

In the patristic period, the communication of news in an angelic encounter was thought to have taken place, initially, at a well. The *Protoevangelium of James*, an ancient Jewish-Christian writing that may include authentic memories from the early community, presumes a first encounter at the well or on the way to the well, with the Annunciation proper taking place in the house of Mary when the Virgin has returned with her water supply. The same is true of the early apocryphal gospel known to modern scholars as "Pseudo-Matthew." The Lutheran philologist and biblical geographer Gustaf Dalman, not an easy man to fool, was willing to credit this as "early tradition."[10] A church built over a well—recorded as providing the water of Nazareth in the seventh century—lies near the town, if outside it. As described by Arculf, who visited it in 670 during a tour of the holy places, the "well-church" was dedicated to the Archangel Gabriel. It was "taken for granted that the angel appeared to Mary at the well."[11] This well-church is to be distinguished from the Christian basilica associated with the house of Mary, the church of the Annunciation with its rocky grotto under the high altar and inscribed with the words *Verbum caro factum*. That phrase sums up the profoundest meaning of the Annunciation event: "The Word was made flesh" (John 1:14).

Before there was an actual liturgical feast of the Annunciation, celebrated on March 25, the Western Liturgy already dwelt on the Annunciation mystery in the build-up to Christmas. The great early twentieth century liturgical scholar Abbot Ildefonso Schuster wrote of the first Sunday of the Advent season: "Unlike the old sacramentaries, in which the year begins with the feast of Christmas, the Roman Missal enters today upon her liturgical cycle."[12] The order of the Roman Missal corresponds, he wrote, to this "lofty conception of history, by which the Incarnation is made the true central event in the world's drama."[13] Perhaps in reaction to the heresy of Nestorianism, which denied the perfect unity of Godhead and manhood in Jesus Christ, a season of preparation for the mystery of the Nativity made its appearance in the West, beginning (or so it would seem) in Ravenna. Abbot Schuster considered the four Advent sermons of St. Peter Chrysologus to be the high point in the pre-Christmas preaching of the ancient Church. In an Advent sermon on the Annunciation, Peter Chrysologus told the faithful at Ravenna, "Through the curse she incurred Eve brought pains upon the wombs of women in childbirth. Now, in this very matter of motherhood, Mary, through the blessing she received, rejoices, is honored, is exalted. Now too, woman-kind has truly become the mother of those who live through grace, just as previously she was the mother of those who by nature are subject to death."[14] Advent, wrote Schuster, who was inspired by these homilies, is a season "full of the joyful announcement of approaching freedom," with the character of "holy enthusiasm, tender gratitude, and an intense longing for the coming of the Word of God in the hearts of all the children of Adam."[15] This Ravenna version of Advent preparation was not exactly a draft of the Roman practice; one respect in which this is so lies in its more accentuated Marian character.

> It is a matter of two types of preparation for Christmas which arose indepen-
> dently: one, more Christological-Marian and at the same time more Historical
> (in the sense of referring to the historical facts that accompanied and mani-
> fested the Incarnation), appears in the West at Ravenna and in the East notably
> in the Syrian church; the other, of a more Christological-eschatological kind,
> has its origins in the churches of Spain and Gaul. This second type of prepara-
> tion for Christmas had an especially important development towards the mid-
> dle of the sixth century when it was accepted at Rome and became an integral
> part of that Roman rite which precisely then began its extraordinary diffusion
> in the West.[16]

The Hispanic-Gaulish-Roman Advent was as much concerned with Christ's second Coming as with his first.

Meanwhile at Milan, the Ambrosian liturgy chose to celebrate the Annun-ciation on Advent's fourth and final Sunday. The practice was taken into the Roman Lectionary in 1969 and has a lingering echo in the texts of the remaining pre-Christmas days. The liturgical revisers of the Roman rite wanted to stress in this way the special place of the Annunciation in Advent time.[17] Previously, the Gospel of the Annunciation was read at Rome only on the first of the Advent Ember days (though these were days of especially intense prayer), with a resonance on the Sunday following in the shape of the antiphon sung at the Offertory.[18]

Once the feast of the Annunciation was established in its own right, it attracted great devotion. For the medieval English, it was "Lady Day" and the real beginning of civil society's New Year. In the Greek Church, though "the Byzantine tradition admits of no feast during Lent, except on Saturdays, the Trullan Synod (692) made an exception for the Annunciation, which is commemorated even if it occurs during the Easter triduum."[19] In the East, Good Friday and the Annunciation can thus be celebrated on the same day. That is significant, as the English theologian John Saward has pointed out in a study of what he terms the "mysteries of March."[20] In the West, a connexion between Annunciation and Atonement is intimated not so much in any calendar as by sacred art—thanks to the "Lily Crucifix" (believed to have been especially common in medieval England), which relates the two mysteries to each other. The lily Gabriel carries to signify his awe at the Virgin's purity appears again, at the artists' hands, on the Cross of her Child, the Innocent Victim of Calvary, here shown as a flowering tree.

How did the great masters of theology see the Annunciation? In the language of St. Thomas, *ingressus*—the entry of the Word on his incarnate life—is what concerns us now. For Aquinas this "entry" spans the entire period from Jesus's Conception until his Baptism in the Jordan, moving via his Birth and Circumcision to the goal of the Baptism, which event is also the initiation of the public ministry. In terms of the liturgical structure of his day and our own, Thomas's *ingressus* thus coincides liturgically with the feast of the Annunciation when taken together with the season of Christmastide. Jesus's Conception is the first event of his human life, and not just the first in a sequence but the first in significance too since it makes possible the series as a whole. To understand his Conception with the mind of the Councils—which means with the mind of the biblical writers as the Fathers of the Church declare it to us—this is already to see in dramatic form who Christ actually is. In Thomas's *Summa theologiae*, all that has preceded by way of teasing out the meaning of the teaching of the Councils about Christ's unique being is now brought to bear on this intimate yet world-changing event: the beginning of Mary of Nazareth's motherhood.

Mary's greatest title, as proclaimed at the Council of Ephesus, the third of the Ecumenical Councils, sums it up: she is the *Theotokos*, the woman who brought forth God. She conceived biologically one who is personally divine. As the Creed tells us, her Child was conceived of the Virgin by the Holy Spirit. Thomas says that the Word assumed our humanity "materially from Mary, but effectively from the Holy Spirit," and by this he means with the Holy Spirit as active cause of our Lady's act of conception.[21]

He will go on to explain that the entire Holy Trinity was involved in this action since God is one. But he adds that the distinctive personal character of the Holy Spirit, as disclosed to us in revelation, makes it highly appropriate to ascribe this event especially to him, the Third Divine Person, as its efficient (or effective) cause. Thomas has several reasons for saying as much, but the most important is the one he places first in his discussion. The Incarnation was the fruit of the mutual love of the Father and the Son—and the Holy Spirit is the expression in God of that selfsame love.[22]

Balthasar too sees the Annunciation as a Trinitarian event, expressed in three reactions of Mary to the threefold salutation of Gabriel.

> The decisive factor is that the angel's three salutations (the first manifesting the Father, the second the Son and the third the Holy Spirit) are each followed

by a reaction on Mary's part, not empty speculation about God but her reflection as to the best possible response and course of action in view of what God has told her. Her reaction to the revelation of the Father is alarm (as, indeed, every creature must be alarmed to be in the immediate presence of God) as she wonders "what sort of greeting this might be," i.e. what it implies in terms of her response and her willingness to be of service. Her second reaction, in the wake of the revelation of the Son whom she is to bear, who will be both God's Son and David's heir, is even more concrete: she asks what practical steps she must take to render the obedience expected of her. Thirdly, in response to the revelation of the Spirit who will overshadow her, she consents to God's perfect Word which is to take effect in her, control her and become flesh in and from her.[23]

The love that guides the Annunciation event bears the mark of the Holy Trinity inasmuch as it is a renunciatory love—and since, in the Trinitarian processions, Omnipotence has made sacrifice its own proper mode, the Father giving himself away to the Son in the Holy Spirit, it is likely, for that very reason, to be a fruitful love, an efficacious love. In the Annunciation moment, the Son does not abandon his divine attributes but, in his incarnate condition, those divine attributes will take on a "different mode," without the Son "losing any of his own nature."[24] Such fruitful kenosis is what divine Goodness is most like. In his book on the Mysteries of the Rosary, Balthasar looked ahead from the Annunciation to the Passion of Christ. The goodness of the Father, made known at the Annunciation

> has already given itself eternally to the Son and to the common Spirit of both; and therefore it can express itself to the world only in a triune manner: through the consent, indeed the offering of himself, of the Son, to make this goodness of the Father known effectively—even unto death on the cross; through the consent and self-offering of the spirit ready to be engaged wholly in the service of this prodigal love of the Father in the self-surrender of the Son.[25]

This, then, is whence the offer comes to which the answering response is made on Israel's behalf by the Virgin Mary. She gives her consent in that perfect mode of active receptivity befitting her whom the Lucan angel has just greeted as "full of grace" (Luke 1:28).

Bulgakov also looked ahead—but to the mysteries of the Nativity and Baptism—"Epiphany"—and Pentecost.

> The Annunciation, "the beginning of our salvation," is also the beginning of the Epiphany, for it pre-reveals the salvific action of the entire Holy Trinity through the Holy Spirit sent from the Father, the conception of the Son of God from the Virgin. This day is also an anticipation of Pentecost, for in the person of the One full of grace [the Mother of God] creation has been deemed worthy of receiving in it the Holy Spirit.[26]

What of the Annunciation in iconographic art (aside from the Lily Crucifix already mentioned)? Its main lines were established as early as the second century in an image in the Roman catacomb of St. Priscilla. The subsequent tradition unfolds certain possibilities in the encounter of the main figures. Most Byzantine icons portray the archangel in swift motion, on legs suggestive of someone running. In his left hand he holds a staff, for he is a messenger, while his right hand stretches out toward the Virgin. She is either sitting, so as to emphasize her superiority to the angel, or standing, so as to stress how she is disposed for God, waiting on his word. She has been occupied, not idling. She may be holding yarn for making thread, or, less frequently, a scroll for reading.

The Orthodox iconographer Leonid Ouspensky counted three main ways artists have painted the relation between the angel and the Mother of God. The first way stresses her "perturbation and fear"; sometimes she drops the thread she is spinning. The second expresses her "perplexity and prudence"; she holds up a hand with the palm facing outward, a sign that as yet there is only the question, "How shall this be?" (Luke 1:34a). [27] Finally, she can be portrayed as bowing her head and pressing her palm to her breast in a gesture of submission. These three ways are also consecutive moments. They are in fact the three phases of the Virgin's reaction to the angel as explained by Balthasar. Taken together—and they can be combined in a single icon—they give expression to the Annunciation episode in its dramatic course. The Mother of God thus "turns Her hand in the direction of the Angel, asking for an answer to the doubts assailing Her and at the same time, by bowing Her head, expresses Her submission."[28] She and the angel do not so much look at each other as look upward, their gaze held by descending rays of light that symbolize the coming of the Holy Spirit. Typically, so Ouspensky notes, the color scheme of these icons intimates a deep inner joy.

The mystery of the Annunciation becomes "ours" only in the sense that it is the presupposition of mysteries that, in no qualified sense, are truly ours as well as Christ's. Yet it is a mystery that, precisely as the presupposition of the mysteries to come, generates joy.

NOTES

1. "[G]enealogies can serve different purposes and . . . an individual can be accorded two or more different genealogies according to the purpose for which they were drawn up," Raymond E. Brown, *The Birth of the Messiah: A Commentary on the Infancy Narratives in Matthew and Luke* (New York: Image Books, 1979 [1977]), 65.

2. Brown, *The Birth of the Messiah*, 65. Brown points out how this prophecy in Genesis is archetypically fulfilled in the visit of the magi to Bethlehem in Matthew 2.

3. Bargil Pixner, O. S. B., *With Jesus through Galilee according to the Fifth Gospel*, 14–19.

4. Marie-Joseph Lagrange, O. P., *Evangile selon saint Matthieu* (Paris: Gabalda, 1948, 8th edition), 2–3.

5. Raymond E. Brown, *The Birth of the Messiah*, 91, fn 72.

6. Brown, *The Birth of the Messiah*, 74.

7. Brown, *The Birth of the Messiah*, 74.

8. Marie-Joseph Lagrange, *Evangile selon saint Matthieu*, 10.

9. Martin Hengel, *The Septuagint as Christian Scripture* (Edinburgh: T. & T. Clark, 2002); see also Mogens Müller, *The First Bible of the Church: A Plea for the Septuagint* (Sheffield: Sheffield Academic Press, 1996).

10. Gustaf Dalman, *Sacred Sites and Ways: Studies in the Topography of the Gospels* (London: SPCK, 1935), 66.

11. Dalman, *Sacred Sites and Ways*, 66.

12. Ildefonso Schuster, *The Sacramentary (Liber Sacramentorum): Historical and Liturgical Notes on the Roman Missal* (London: Burns, Oates and Washbourne, 1924), I., 319.

13. Schuster, *The Sacramentary*, 319.

14. Peter Chrysologus, *Sermon* 140. See Peter Chrysologus, *Selected Sermons* (New York: Fathers of the Church, Inc., 1953), 228.

15. Ildefonso Schuster, *The Sacramentary*, I. 320.

16. Franco Sottocornola, *L'Anno liturgico nei sermoni di Pietro Crisologo* (Cesena: Centro studi e ricerche sulla antica provincia ecclesiastica ravennate, 1973), 254–55.

17. Irénée-Henri Dalmais, Pierre Jounel, and Aimé Georges Martimort, *The Church at Prayer, An Introduction to the Liturgy, IV: The Liturgy and Time* (London: Chapman, 1986), 95–96.

18. The Ember Days began as Roman civic festivals to mark the beginning of spring, summer, autumn, and winter, and in the Church were kept as days of ascetical preparation for the Sundays held to initiate the seasons, and for the ordinations of priests and deacons.

19. Irénée-Henri Dalmais, Pierre Jounel, and Aimé Georges Martimort, *The Church at Prayer, An Introduction to the Liturgy, IV: The Liturgy and Time*, 96.

20. John Saward, *The Mysteries of March: Hans Urs von Balthasar on the Incarnation and Easter* (London: Collins, 1990).

21. Thomas Aquinas, *Summa theologiae*, IIIa., q. 32, a. 3, ad iii.

22. Aquinas, IIIa., q. 32, a. 1, corpus.

23. Hans Urs von Balthasar, *Prayer*, (San Francisco, CA: Ignatius, 1986), 193–94.

24. Thus Balthasar's curious metaphor of the *Hinterlegung* or "depositing" of the Son's divinity with the Father as explained in Martin Bieler, "God and the Cross," art. cit., 81.

25. Hans Urs von Balthasar, *The Threefold Garland* (Et San Francisco: Ignatius, 1982), 28.

26. Sergius Bulgakov, *Churchly Joy : Orthodox Devotions for the Church Year* (Grand Rapids, MI: Eerdmans, 2008), 80.

27. Vladimir Lossky and Leonid Ouspensky, *The Meaning of Icons* (Crestwood, NY: St. Vladimir's Seminary Press, 1982), 172.

28. Lossky and Ouspensky, *The Meaning of Icons*, 172.

Chapter Six

Nativity

Lagrange wrote a popular summary of his four great commentaries on the Gospels. There he informs his readers how in the year 9 "Before the Common Era" the then proconsul of Roman Asia had made a proposal to his province. The birthday of Augustus should be the start of its New Year since Augustus's birth was "the source of all our benefit."[1] It was a suggestion that suited the growing emperor cult of the age. And Lagrange comments, à propos of the infancy gospel of Luke that shows such interest in naming those in power at the time of Jesus's birth,

> Is it St Luke's intention, then to imitate the official protocol? Perhaps; but if he does so it is with a tremendous difference. It was rather his intention to accept the challenge thrown down by these proud monarchs or by their flattering courtiers when he claimed the title of Saviour for a Child born in a crib, a Child who at that time had few to pay Him homage. And events have proved that Luke was in the right, for it is from the birth-day of Jesus that we count this new era, the Christian era, which, by contrast with that unknown time when the world first came into being is like a new creation.[2]

The rationale for the birth at Bethlehem is given in Luke's Gospel itself. Davidides needed to be present in the city of David at the time of a census. The claims of the traditional grotto site, a low-lying room on the south side of the early Christian basilica of the Nativity in that town, struck Dalman as plausible enough. Local practice was unlikely to have changed much, though nearly two millennia had passed. For peasants, economic and social conditions in the Late Ottoman period—near whose end Dalman did his research—were much the same as what they had been in Late Antiquity. The "stable" would have been for donkeys and cows rather than horses (horses were fed in the open air) with the food placed in the manger, in a flat trough or a "niche with a deepened floor . . . built into the wall for this purpose."[3] The "manger" would have combined a rocky shelf with sides made from clay. Not unnaturally, the earthen sides have since disappeared. If the grotto were a dwelling for humans, with animal space adjoining, then the difference in floor level notable at the church of the Nativity fits well enough. Dalman takes St. Luke to be saying in his Gospel (at Luke 2:7) that the inn lacked *suitable* room—that is, there was no room fit for a birth with a bed for the baby. As to the inn itself, "[s]uch a guesthouse is a public place, where no one has the right to be alone."[4] What Mary and Joseph were shown was a cave dwelling instead. So remarks the second century writer St. Justin who knew Palestine well and was aware of how common caves were. Justin saw in this contingency a fulfillment of a prophecy in the Book of Isaiah: the righteous King will "dwell in a high cave of a mighty rock," which is the Septuagint version of Isaiah 33:16.[5]

What of the angelophany in the "Shepherds' Fields," the music and voices heard by local herders at the time the birth was happening? Tradition, just because it flows from and also incorporates Scripture, has no difficulty in accommodating the existence of separated intelligences and their capacity to make use of sensuous media in a ministry to human beings. That *music*, specifically, should be heard is consonant with the messianic joy foretold by prophetic oracles like Zephaniah 3:14–20. The Latin doctor St. Jerome, who moved to Bethlehem in the late fourth century, had described a visit by his Roman friend St. Paula to what was already by then the traditional site, a "flock-tower" situated a short distance from the little city. Dalman comments:

> The low-lying shepherds' plain must be taken as the place nearest to Bethlehem where scarcely any snow falls in winter, and where in the case of need flocks can remain at night in the open; for the great drop in temperature which sometimes occurs in the winter generally makes itself felt only after Christmas. St. Luke did not think of winter in his narrative, but it is clear that the place chosen by tradition corresponds to his purpose.[6]

Here Dalman found another fulfillment of messianic prophecy, this time from the Book of Micah. "And you, O daughter of Zion, dark tower of the flock, on you it will come and enter in (Micah 4:8)." This "remote flock-tower east of Bethlehem," he wrote, "was to be enwrapt in the messianic glory."[7] True, the setting for what the shepherds heard that night could in theory have been any of the valleys round Bethlehem. Yet,

> as we have no clue to guide us, fellowship is not to be despised with the thousands of Christians who, since the fourth century have listened in spirit with contemplation and longing to the Christmas hymn of the angels here among the olive-groves of the church of the Shepherds.[8]

The birth has been celebrated from ancient times. Keeping the feast of the Nativity on December 25 seems to have begun in Rome and to have spread via Antioch to Constantinople, and from there to Jerusalem and Alexandria, thus encompassing all the main centers of early Christianity, the seats of the eventual patriarchates. St. John Chrysostom, who introduced the feast at Antioch around 375, was under the impression that the actual records of the census in which Mary and Joseph participated were still held at Rome and preserved the date of Jesus's birth. That can hardly be so. Most likely, there was a different reason for the choice of day. Referring to a calendar made in the fourth century by Furius Dionysius Philocalus, Abbot Schuster wrote,

> The civil calendar of the Philocalian compilation gives on December 25 the *Natalis invicti*—that is to say, the birthday of the sun, which thus coincides exactly with the winter solstice. In an age when, through the Mithraic mysteries, the worship of the golden orb of day had assumed such proportions that, according to St Leo, the very same worshippers who frequented the Vatican Basilica allowed themselves also to practise the superstitious custom of first saluting the solar disc in the atrium of St Peter's, it is not unlikely that the Apostolic See, in anticipating our Lord's birthday on December 25, intended to oppose the *Sol invictus*, Mithras, to the true Sun of Justice, desiring in this way to turn away the faithful from the dangerous idolatry of the Mithraic festivals.[9]

The connection is borne out by the fact that the "oldest Christian mosaic in Rome, the one in the mausoleum of the Julii in the cemetery on the Vatican, shows Christ the sun in his triumphal chariot."[10] It dates from the mid third century.

The Latin Liturgy, like the Latin Fathers, bring the Nativity drama under the heading of *admirabile commercium*, a "wonderful exchange." In the Christmas season, the Roman Office has several antiphons that teach the doctrine of the exchange. That is notably so on the Octave Day of Christmas, kept in the *Vetus Ordo* (before 1969) as the feast of the Circumcision, but in the *Novus Ordo* (after that date) as the "Solemnity of Mary, Mother of God." At First Vespers on that day, the Latin Church (old or new) sings, "O wonderful exchange! The Creator of human nature took on a human body, and was born of the Virgin. He became man without having a human father and has bestowed on us the divine nature."[11] In this exchange, the Word comes to teach and by his example to heal spiritual ailments. But he also does more. He confers on human beings the right to share an eternal inheritance, opening up to them friendship with God. In the fifth century, St. Leo, in his sermons on the Nativity, offered both encouragement and warning: "O Christian, recognize your dignity. And having been made a sharer in Divinity, take care not to the fall away from so sublime a state."[12] The dignity turns not just on the fact of the Incarnation. The baptized, through the faith whereby they adhere to the Word, actually come to share in the wonderful exchange in which the Incarnation consists. Thus St. Gregory the Great could write in the first of his *Homilies on the Gospels*, "As Divinity accepted the weakness of our flesh, so human flesh received the Light that pardoned it. Truly God having suffered human things, man was thereby lifted up to divine things."[13]

The Nativity feast, then, concerns not only, for the Latin Fathers, the doctrine of the Incarnation but also a teaching on the deification of the redeemed. The grace of Christmas concerns not simply *enanthropesis*—"hominisation"—for God, but what their Greek counterparts would term *theosis*—"divinization"—for men. The key lies in the "Secret" Prayer (in more recent parlance, the "Prayer over the Gifts") in the Roman-rite Mass of Midnight. That prayer asks that "we may grow to be like him in whom our human nature is one with Thine."[14] In an obvious sense, imitation of Christ would be impossible without his birth. But that impossibility is not just on the level of logic. It is also on the level of "onto-logic"—the logic of being, and not just the logic of thought. In the birth of Christ, God took upon himself our human nature in order to give us a share, by participatory likeness, in his divine nature. So what transpires at the Nativity is, as Abbot Marmion remarks, "a divine-human exchange. The child born on Christmas Day is at the same time God, and the human nature that God takes to himself from us is to serve as the instrument through which he communicates his divinity to us."[15] Likewise, among the Greek Fathers, while the preeminent theologian of the Greek Church, St. Gregory Nazianzen, places his chief emphasis on the life and work of Jesus, he still identifies the Birth as the foundational event of our restoration: "[T]he *enanthropesis* of the Son was the very means by which the "cure" for mankind's disease was effected." [16] Like the Annunciation, the Nativity is our mystery at the very least in the sense that it is the essential precondition for our reception of the succeeding mysteries of Christ.

Yet for Pope Leo, simply to qualify the mystery of the Nativity as a presupposition of further mysteries (which can *genuinely* become ours) would be a serious underestimate. For St. Augustine, to remember the Birth of Christ was a *memoria*, a "commemoration," but for St. Leo it is the *sacramentum Nativitatis Christi*, where simple meditation on that Birth, feasible in principle on any day of the year, takes on a different character.[17] "The *virtus operis* of the acts of Christ is operative on this [Christmas] day as in every celebration of the *sacramentum salutis* since the Son of God became man so as to make us share in his divinity."[18] "If the event is past, the virtue and the efficacy of the mystery remain."[19] That power and effectiveness were in the Head, and now they are to be in the members where they will contribute to our remaking in the divine image that was spoiled in Adam. For this, the celebration of the Nativity, on its proper festival, must be carried out *legitime*—which means for Leo "leading a life . . . in conformity with the mystery celebrated, and sharing in the mysteries of Christ no longer only in their *sacramentum* but in their *exemplum*," walking henceforth in newness of life, as befits the regenerated, those who are born again.[20]

> No doubt this state of childhood which the majesty of the Son of God was not ashamed to inhabit, developed little by little till the age of perfect manhood; no doubt he consummated the triumph of his Passion and Resurrection; and all the acts of the humble condition he assumed for us belong to the past. And yet, the present feast of Jesus born of the Virgin Mary renews for us these sacred beginnings, and while we adore the Nativity of our Lord, we find ourselves celebrating our own origin: the Birth of Christ, indeed, is the beginning of the Christian people, and the birthday of the Head is that of the body. What does it matter if the elect are called each in turn, that all the children of the Church are spread out in the succession of times! It is the totality of the faithful, issuing from the baptismal fountain, which, crucified with Christ in his Passion, risen in his Resurrection, placed at the Father's right at his Ascension, is today also in this Nativity co-engendered with him.[21]

The co-engendering is renewed in Christians by contemplation of the Nativity, above all in its liturgical celebration, and the consequence is spiritual joy.

How do Thomas and the later masters see it? Thomas is guided in his reflections by his knowledge of the Councils of Ephesus and Chalcedon. In what sense is an uncreated Person—the Person of the Word who always was in God—be "born"? Birth can be thought of in two ways, says Aquinas, with regard to the "subject" born, and in relation to the "term" of the birth in question. At the Nativity of Christ the hypostasis of the Word is born (this, on Thomas's view, is required by Chalcedon), but the divine nature is not engendered. The term of this birth is exclusively the human nature the Word has assumed. But "to speak properly, the nature does not begin to exist, it is rather the Person who begins to exist in a nature."[22] Following Cyril of Alexandria (the master theologian of Ephesus), "One says that he was born according to the flesh, because, for us and our salvation, he united to himself, according to hypostasis, what is human and came forth from woman."[23] "The blessed Virgin is Mother of God, not because she was mother of the divinity, but because she is mother, according to the humanity, of this person who possesses both divinity and humanity."[24] The Word is not different after the Incarnation than he was before, yet there has been a real change—it exists in the motherly relation between Mary and the Word, thanks to the human nature assumed.[25] Thomas goes on to make his own the teaching of the Lateran Synod, which preceded the Sixth Ecumenical Council. In this birth there was no rupture of the hymen as the baby came from the womb; Mary suffered no pain, but only joy, according to the prophecy of Isaiah: "[The desert] shall blossom abundantly, and rejoice with joy and singing" (Isaiah 35:2).

For Balthasar the assumption of human nature must be considered in its implications for the Word who now exists and acts in a human life like our own as well as in the nature he shares with Father and Spirit. Seen thus it can only be called an "infinite plunge."[26]

> Perhaps the triune plan looked rather different when it was conceived in eternal life, where the meaning and goal of the whole may be surveyed with a single glance; perhaps it looked different from now, when this swaddled Child lies before the eyes of the Father in indistinguishable ordinariness, in this stall exposed to all the winds of human indifference and disdain. But God's Spirit mediates: he has measured the whole road from exaltedness to lowliness and he bears witness to the Father that the descent into unrecognizability corresponds precisely to the triune design.[27]

To repeat the words of that American scholar who sought to depict the common vision of Balthasar and Bulgakov: this "mode of perfect, absolute, self-sacrificial, and ecstatic love, which is constitutive for divine personhood, is that which substantially and essentially is divinity."[28] And now this personal mode of uncreated existence, exemplified in the Trinitarian Son, exists also in time. Bulgakov wrote,

> God becomes incarnate in voluntary self-depletion. . . . He overcomes this infirmity from within, without destroying the human essence; and being true God, He is also true man. And He is born this day in Bethlehem from the Virgin Mary.[29]

What of the icons of Christmas? The Byzantine icons bring together the Birth and the visit of the magi. The developed Byzantine-Slav icon combines with the chief agents—the Savior and his Mother—the shepherds and the magi, and in this it corresponds to the Byzantine Liturgy's *Kontakion* for Christmas Day: "Today the Virgin gives birth to Him who is above all being, and the earth offers a cave to Him whom no man can approach. Angels with shepherds give glory, and Magi journey with a star. For unto us is born a young Child, the pre-eternal God."[30] Two further subsidiary scenes, inspired by early Christian literature, are included in this icon. One, placed at bottom right, shows a couple of midwives brought in by Joseph to wash the newly born Child. It is a vignette that emphasizes the reality of Jesus's humanity. The other additional scene, placed at bottom left, shows Joseph being tempted by the Devil in the form of an old man. Satan aims to sow doubt. He appeals to the law of nature: a virgin birth is impossible. Here it is the uniqueness of Jesus's humanity that is stressed.

As to Mary, the Mother of the Lord, she can be portrayed gazing at her Child, or looking out at the wider world, or as in a Novgorod School icon from the fifteenth century reproduced by Leonid Ouspensky, she may have her eye fixed on her husband, "as if expressing by this look compassion for his state."[31] She may be sitting half upright, indicating the painless nature of the virgin Birth, or lying in a condition of lassitude to show its human reality. In any case she is always central, and frequently larger than the other figures. She lies outside the entrance to the cave where the Child is—but only just outside. As to the angels, some look up, some look down, thus attesting both their God-centeredness and their ministry to men. The shepherds listen to the angelic music, and sometimes join in, one playing a reed pipe, thereby adding human art to angelic sound. Meanwhile, the wise men come walking with their gifts, attracted by the star that the iconographers convey by painting rays of light emerging from an opening in the heavenly world. How they are portrayed indicates who iconographers, or the churches from which they came, thought they were.

AN EXCURSUS ON THE VISIT OF THE MAGI (WESTERN EPIPHANY)

St. Justin, and later St. Epiphanius, both of whom were Palestinians by birth, "tell us that the Magi came from the country on the other side of the Dead Sea, which was all included under the general name of Arabia."[32] In his commentary on St. Matthew's Gospel, Lagrange, here cited, suggests this was the local Palestinian tradition, handed down inter-generationally and deserving of respect.[33] Arabians, who had a number of Jews in their midst, might have known of the prophecy of Balaam (Numbers 24:17) who, as a Moabite, was also from "Arabia." The magi's gifts of gold, frankincense, and myrrh, so Lagrange explained, are typically Arabian gifts. It was those gifts that made the North African ecclesiastical writer Tertullian think they were kings—for had not Psalm 71:10 foretold that *kings* from Arabia and Saba would bring gifts to the Messiah? The Western iconography, building on the Tertullianic inheritance, created a distinct scene of royal magi offering gifts to the infant Jesus, the King to come, seated on Mary's lap. This is not a Nativity scene, yet the One portrayed is still the Jewish Messiah—but now presented in his claim to universal sovereignty as the pagan nations come to do him homage.

Can the Visit of the Magi count as a mystery, rather than just an adjunct of the mystery of the Nativity? At first sight, it can only be a didactic adjunct. Clearly, a lesson is taught to us by the combination of the local and lowly with the grand and exotic. Aquinas, for instance, finds a notable message in the way the manger of the Christ-child was visited by shepherds and magi. In his eyes, these two groups stand respectively not only for the first fruits of the Jews and of the Gentiles but also for the contrast of the simple and the learned. The message touches the catholicity of the Word's aim, and signals the all-inclusiveness intended for the Church that will be his extended Body.[34] But for St. Leo, there was more than this, which turns the Visit, the Western Epiphany, into something closer to a mystery *per se*. The "something more" concerns the continuing immediacy of the proclamation the festival carries, which draws the Latin-style Epiphany into the ambit of the mysteries properly so called. In words of the patrologist Mark Armitage,

> The Christological faith of the magi is not simply a past event, but a mystery present in "the narrative which is read to us from the gospel" (*narratio evangelicae lectionis*) whose power continues to be felt in the here and now. The Epiphany is a present reality because the process—*narratio*—by which God proclaims his salvation to the nations, and by which the nations recognize the redemption offered to them in Jesus Christ, is one which continues in Leo's own day.[35]

For Leo, therefore, the Epiphany is inseparable not just from the Nativity but from Pentecost too.

> At the Nativity, Christ is born and the process by which the nations are built up into the *caelestis Hierusalem* [heavenly Jerusalem] is inaugurated; at the Epiphany, Christ reveals himself to the nations by a graced illumination which leads them to acknowledge his divinity and his humanity; and at Pentecost the church assumes as its own property the languages of the nations, and, by the power of the Spirit, irrigates the earth with Christ's gospel.[36]

And again, "Leo's theology is a *lumen gentium* theology—a theology rooted in the idea that the Nativity and Epiphany represent that moment at which God's salvation is finally and definitively proclaimed to the Gentiles, and that, when the *gentes* recognize and worship the *lumen*, the *caelestis Hierusalem* comes into being."[37] It is a reading of the Western Epiphany as, in the time of the Church, a continuously enacted mystery that looks ahead to the last mysteries considered in this book, Pentecost and the Parousia.

NOTES

1. Marie-Joseph Lagrange, O. P., *The Gospel of Jesus Christ* (London: Burns, Oates and Washbourne, 1938), I. 9
2. Lagrange, *The Gospel of Jesus Christ*, I. 9.
3. Gustaf Dalman, *Sacred Sites and Ways: Studies in the Topography of the Gospels* (London: SPCK, 1935), 40.
4. Dalman, *Sacred Sites and Ways*, 43.
5. Justin Martyr, *Dialogue with Trypho*, 78. 5.
6. Gustaf Dalman, *Sacred Sites and Ways*, 48–49.
7. Dalman, *Sacred Sites and Ways*, 50.
8. Dalman, *Sacred Sites and Ways*, 50.
9. Ildefonso Schuster, *The Sacramentary (Liber Sacramentorum): Historical and Liturgical Notes on the Roman Missal* (London: Burns, Oates and Washbourne, 1924), I., 362.

10. Irénée-Henri Dalmais, Pierre Jounel, and Aimé Georges Martimort, *The Church at Prayer, An Introduction to the Liturgy, IV: The Liturgy and Time*, 78.

11. *The Divine Office: The Liturgy of the Hours according to the Roman Rite. I* (London and Glasgow: Collins, 1974), 247.

12. Leo I, *Sermon* 21.

13. Gregory the Great, *Homily 1 on the Gospels.*

14. *The Missal in Latin and English* (London: Burns, Oates and Washbourne, 1952), 33.

15. Columba Marmion, *Christ in his Mysteries*, (Bethesda, MD: Zacchaeus Press, 2008), 133.

16. Donald F. Winslow, *The Dynamics of Salvation: A Study in Gregory of Nazianzus* (Cambridge, MA: Philadelphia Patristic Foundation, 1979), 90, 91.

17. Jean Gaillard, "Noël, memoria ou mystère?" *Maison-Dieu* 59 (1959), 37–59; compare Leo, *Sermon* 28.

18. Jean Gaillard, "Noël, memoria ou mystère?" art. cit., 47.

19. Marie Bernard de Soos, *Le Mystère liturgique d'après saint Léon le Grand*, (Münster: Aschendorff, 1958), op. cit, 73.

20. De Soos, *Le Mystère liturgique*, 94.

21. Leo, *Sermon* 26.

22. Thomas Aquinas, *Summa theologiae*, IIIa., q. 35, a. 1, ad iii.

23. Aquinas, q. 35, a. 1, ad ii.

24. Aquinas, q. 35, a. 4, ad iii.

25. Aquinas, q. 35, a. 5, corpus.

26. Hans Urs von Balthasar, *The Threefold Garland* (San Francisco, CA: Ignatius, 1982), 48.

27. Hans Urs von Balthasar, *The Threefold Garland*, 48–49.

28. Jennifer Newsome Martin, *Hans Urs von Balthasar and the Critical Appropriation of Russian Religious Thought* (Notre Dame, IN: University of Notre Dame Press, 2015), 190.

29. Sergius Bulgakov, *Churchly Joy Orthodox Devotions for the Church Year* (Grand Rapids, MI: Eerdmans, 2008), 25.

30. Mother Mary and Archimandrite Kallistos Ware (tr.), *The Festal Menaion* (London: Faber and Faber, 1969), 277.

31. Vladimir Lossky and Leonid Ouspensky, *The Meaning of Icons* (Crestwood, NY: St. Vladimir's Seminary Press, 1982), 160.

32. Marie-Joseph Lagrange, O. P., *The Gospel of Jesus Christ* (London: Burns, Oates and Washbourne, 1938), I., 42.

33. Marie-Joseph Lagrange, O. P., *Evangile selon saint Matthieu* (Paris: Gabalda, 1948, 8th edition), 20.

34. Thomas Aquinas, *Summa theologiae* IIIa., q. 36, a. 8, and a. 3; cf. Thomas Aquinas, *Commentary on the Gospel of Matthew* 2, I. lect. 1.

35. J. Mark Armitage, *A Twofold Solidarity* (Strathfield, NSW: St Paul's Publications, 2005), 38. Cf. Marie Bernard de Soos, *Le Mystère liturgique d'après saint Léon le Grand*, 35.

36. J. Mark Armitage, *A Twofold Solidarity*, 38.

37. Armitage, *A Twofold Solidarity*, 37.

Chapter Seven

Baptism

The Baptism is, in Lagrange's expression, the "inauguration of the Messiah."[1] A voice is crying in the desert: the Reign of God is approaching, so the Lord's way must be prepared. Raymond Brown explains:

> Having disclaimed the traditional eschatological roles [Elijah and the Prophet-like-Moses], John the Baptist now identifies himself in the same humble terms by which the Synoptics identify him, namely, as the preparatory voice of Isaiah 40:3. The Isaian passage originally referred to the role of the angels in preparing a way through the desert by which Israel might return from the Babylonian captivity to the land of Palestine. Like a modern bulldozer the angels were to level hills and fill in the valleys, and thus prepare a superhighway. But John the Baptist is to prepare a road, not for God's people to return to the promised land, but for God to come to His people. His baptizing and preaching in the desert was opening up the hearts of men, levelling their pride, filling their emptiness, and thus preparing them for God's intervention. . . . The Qumran Essenes used precisely this text to explain why they chose to live in the desert: they were preparing the way for the Lord by studying and observing the Law.[2]

St. Matthew stresses John's austerity: John lived off locusts and wild honey. The first sounds distinctly unpalatable, but the wild honey was exquisite and much sought after. However, the same word could be used for the exudation of certain trees. The monks of St. Catherine's monastery, Mount Sinai, collected this sap in Lagrange's day, and he tells us its taste was insipid.[3] Pharisees and Sadducees came to him, perhaps just to observe, or otherwise to undergo the rite he performed—inasmuch as they understood it, which may not have been very well. According to Josephus, Pharisees took the ritual ablution to symbolize the pureness of their own souls.

For the evangelist Matthew, John's baptism of Jesus had a purpose alto-
gether unique. In Lagrange's words in his commentary on the First Gospel,

> It is the manifestation of Jesus as one stronger than John, and who must
> replace his baptism by a new baptism in the Spirit. Christian baptism is not yet
> instituted, and John will continue to baptize; but Jesus is invested with his
> mission; already one order is succeeding to another.[4]

Of course there was also something more straightforward, the "baptism of
repentance," which the Pharisees misconstrued as a seal of approval, not a
call for *metanoia*, for conversion of heart. To cite Lagrange again, "in the
same way that [Jesus] submitted to the Law, he accepted the conditions
preliminary to Messianism, of which the chief was a baptism of repentance.
It was a plan of God for an epoch of transition."[5] The transition was to
something utterly new, as St. Mark concurs, presenting John the Baptist's
activity as a prophecy of Jesus's *evangelion*—the "good tidings" of his "advent as King-Messiah."[6] It is as *prophecy of Jesus*, specifically, that John the
Forerunner binds together the ancient covenants and the New. The baptism
of repentance that he celebrated was above all a "baptism of messianic preparation."[7] In the New Testament volume of his theological aesthetics, Balthasar writes of the Baptist:

> He, like all those sent, does not know who he is—all the more is this true,
> since his mission is the greatest that anyone born of woman has received
> (Matthew11:11), and therefore the least surveyable. He knows only his com-
> mission, to be a voice that calls (in reality a voice that is called) in the wilder-
> ness: "Clear the path of the Lord."[8]

And he adds of the Baptized,

> Jesus' descent into the river is at one and the same time solidarity with all who
> confess their guilt and dive into the waters of judgment and salvation, and—as
> solidarity—obedience to the voice of God which sounds forth from the proph-
> et's voice, and thus obedience incarnated in history. Jesus' initiative attains
> immediately to its fulfillment, for he "rises up" out of the waters, and his act of
> "coming up from beneath" is answered by the "coming down from above" of
> the "Spirit (of God)": here we see that incarnation is the encounter, to the point
> of identification, of the Israel who has been made ready and the God of the
> covenant who descends to Israel.[9]

In this way, the Baptism of the Lord bears witness to the two natures of the
Word incarnate, human and divine, in their perfect union, without separation
but without confusion, joined as they are in his unique person. It also testifies
to the Holy Trinity. The Spirit of God, issuing from the Father of the Son, is
"the culminating eschatological gift for the humanity of the One who has

become man."[10] This has an "economic" aim, an aim in the achieving of salvation for the world, for forwarding God's work of salvation among humankind as a whole. "In the Anointing the Father lets the Spirit come on the Son who for his part gives the Spirit again so that the Spirit may be active on the creature and lead it, through bonding with Christ, to the Father."[11]

In the patristic age, this *Theophania* or "Manifestation of God," was included within the wider "epiphanic" set of events stretching from the Visit of the Magi via the Baptism in the Jordan to the first of the Lord's "signs," worked at Cana in Galilee.

> Epiphany means "appearance" or "manifestation," and among the Eastern Christians had originally the same significance as Christmas in Rome. It was the festival of the eternal Word, clothed in the flesh, revealing himself to mankind. Three different phases of this historical manifestation were especially venerated—viz., the adoration of the Magi at Bethlehem, the changing of the water into wine at Cana, and the baptism of Jesus in the Jordan. [12]

But in age of the Fathers, the liturgical celebration of the Baptism in particular was complicated by questions of use and abuse. Schuster makes the claim that, as early as the Letters of St. John, Gnostic Christology found in the episode of the Baptism the moment when the divine nature became united with Jesus's human nature, to abandon it again at the Crucifixion. (Hence John's counter-affirmation, "Jesus Christ came by water and blood, not with the water only but with the water and the blood" [I John 5:6].) In the early patristic period, St. Irenaeus appears to have defined his view of what transpired at the Jordan "over against an interpretation of the Baptism for which the reception of the Spirit was considered endowment with divinity, such that the higher pneumatic Christ came down upon the psychic Jesus of the Demiurge which whom Christ was united until, on the way to Pontius Pilate, he withdrew again into the pneumatic Pleroma of the Aeons."[13] That kind of thinking among the unorthodox suggested to Schuster a countervailing desire among the orthodox to "set against the Gnostic baptismal manifestation the temporal birth at Bethlehem."[14]

This would explain how, at least in the West, the Epiphany feast came to have so complex a history. On the one hand, the Gospel events of the Baptism—and the Marriage-feast at Cana—were definitely included, along with the Visit of the Magi. On the other hand, there was also a tendency to treat the Jordan and Cana events as secondary in comparison to the Bethlehem events, the events of the Birth. In Rome, at any rate, "the historical recurrence of the Nativity of our Lord came to occupy so prominent a place in the popular mind that it is still the predominating idea throughout the whole of the Christmas Liturgy."[15] There the ancient feast of the "Manifestation," kept on January 6, retained its place—but it lost its full significance. The shadow—or radiance—of the Nativity festival on December 25 was too strong for it. The "Crib of Bethlehem," owing to its "power of attraction," gave greater prominence to the Visit of the Magi, which thus became the heart of the Western Epiphany.[16] The Baptism in the Jordan, once the centerpiece of the Manifestation, was displaced in the West. It was not, however, mislaid entirely. The Roman church of the third century was "still faithfully following the primitive Eastern tradition and administering solemn baptism on the date of the *Theophania*."[17] When in due course the Western feast of the Epiphany was given an Octave, or eight-day celebration, the Octave-day was assigned for its Gospel reading the Baptism of the Lord and the antiphons of the day were translated from the Greek (at Charlemagne's request).[18] Eventually the Greek church too would cease to set aside the *Theophania* for the baptism of new disciples. After adult Baptisms became rare and Byzantine babies and infants began to be baptized at home, a solemn blessing of the waters took its place. In Orthodox practice today, a priest "dips a cross into the water three times before setting it on a platform that is adorned with flowers. Each person present approaches, kisses the cross, is sprinkled with the holy water and takes a sip of it. After the service each may draw some water from the container and keep it at home."[19] So a Western liturgist describes the current ceremonial.

What did the great theologians make of it? Emphasis on the Baptism as Theophany would suit the Christology of Aquinas. For St. Thomas, by whose time Gnosticism was only in the memory of learned clerks, the Baptism of Christ in the Jordan begins the deep mysteries. The emphasis shifts from presupposition of the historic revelation (the Annunciation, the Nativity) or major event in that revelation (the Visit of the Magi) to a mystery involving Christians directly. No longer, as with such mysteries of the Infancy as the Western Epiphany, is it just a matter of instruction about the divine plan. Here Thomas was faithful to the patristic witnesses he had to hand. The texts of the Fathers gave him the confidence to say how it was fitting for Christ to receive the baptism of John because his descent into the waters opened the way for Jesus's own disciples to receive the Baptism of Christ.[20] It was not just that Jesus wished to show he approved John's practice of a baptism of repentance, which could count as preparation for his own public ministry—though he did—and Thomas could cite St. Bede to this effect. But more than that was at stake. In St. Ambrose's words as cited by Thomas, "The Lord was baptized not because he wished to be cleansed by the waters, but in order to cleanse them, that, having been purified by the flesh of Christ that knew no sin, they might assume the power of Baptism."[21] Thomas backs up this citation with another text, this time from the unknown author whose commentary on the Gospel according to St. Matthew was passed down under the name of St. John Chrysostom. The Savior was baptized so that "he might bequeath the [thus] sanctified waters to those who would be baptized afterwards."[22] The fourth century Cappadocian Father St. Gregory Nazianzen added, so Thomas recalls, "Christ was baptized in order that he might plunge in the water the old Adam in his entirety."[23]

So it is a mystery of Christ which is to become the mystery of Christians, even though as yet Thomas does not bring into play his full vocabulary for how this can actually happen. The heavens were opened, he says, keeping close to the language of the Gospels and the Fathers, at Christ's Baptism in the Jordan, so as to show that for the future divine power would be at work in our own Baptism, gateway as it is for the sacramental life.[24] It was right that the Father's voice was heard pointing out Christ and that the Spirit was seen as a dove descending on him, for the whole Trinity will be active in our own baptismal regeneration. As Thomas puts it, "what is accomplished in our baptism should be manifested in Christ's baptism, which was the exemplar of ours."[25]

This claim receives robust expression in the Byzantine tradition. Commenting on the texts of the Theophany, the English translators of the *Festal Menaion* explain:

> [W]hen Christ "went down into the Jordan, as the New Adam he carried us sinful men down with Him: and there in the waters He cleansed us, bearing each of us up once more out of the river as a new creature, regenerate and reconciled. In Christ's baptism at the hands of John, our own baptismal regeneration is already accomplished by anticipation. The many celebrations of the Eucharist are all a participation in the single and unique Last Supper; and in a similar way all our individual baptisms are a sharing in the baptism of Christ—they are the means whereby the 'grace of Jordan' is extended so that it may be appropriated by each one of us personally."[26]

We have already heard Balthasar on this subject, writing on the biblical foundation of approach to this mystery in *The Glory of the Lord*, so let us turn for the later masters to Bulgakov instead. In his "The Open Heavens: Oration on the Epiphany," Bulgakov relates the mystery of the Baptism both to the mystery of the Nativity, and to the sacramental life of the redeemed, who are cleansed in the baptismal waters of Christ's Church.

> If the Birth of Christ was the first Epiphany of the Son of God, who by His becoming man manifested obedience to the Father in his Divinity, then His Baptism became the definitive Epiphany, in which the God-man manifested obedience to the Father also in His humanity.[27]

Bulgakov goes on to say that just as the entire divine Trinity was involved in that Baptism, so it must be likewise in the sacramental expression of that Baptism that is the "christening" of the faithful, enacted as the latter is in the power of the Trinitarian Name.

What of the icons of the Baptism? As with the Nativity icon, the segment of a circle indicates the opening heavens from which rays descend onto the Savior, with the dove of the Holy Spirit taking the place of the magi's star. St. John Damascene, as other Fathers, describes the Theophany in the light of the ending of the Flood in the Genesis prehistory. "[J]ust as then the world was purified of its iniquities by the water of the Flood and the dove brought an olive branch into Noah's Ark, announcing the end of the Flood and peace returned upon earth, so too now the Holy Spirit comes down in the form of a dove to announce the remission of sins and God's mercy to the world. 'There an olive branch, here the mercy of our God,' says St. John of Damascus."[28] Christ is shown standing with water as a background, as in a cave, a way of signifying his total immersion since the Baptism foreshadowed his saving Death, a total experience. To indicate his initiative he is shown as gesturing or even walking towards John the Baptist while also inclining his head to below the level of John's arm. With his right hand he blesses the Jordan waters, which henceforth will be an image of life, not death. The Baptist places his right hand on the Savior's head, and with the other either holds a scroll, symbolizing his preaching, or makes a gesture of prayer, signifying the awe that has come over him. Following indicators in the Byzantine Liturgy angels attend, their hands covered by their cloaks in a sign of reverence, or, in some icons, hold out clothing for when the Savior comes out of the water. Ouspensky explains the additional figures in the river, one male, the other female, down among the fish in the watery depths.[29] They illustrate Psalm 113:3, read as a prophecy rather than simply a verse from a historical psalm. "The sea saw and fled; Jordan was turned back." The female represents the Sea of Reeds, crossed by Israel in the Exodus from Egypt. The male figure represents the Jordan, whose waters parted for Joshua and Elisha. These Old Testament events thus become, in an iconographic expression of Tradition's interpretation of Scripture, types of the Baptism of the Lord.

NOTES

1. Marie-Joseph Lagrange, *Evangile selon saint Matthieu* (Paris: Gabalda, 1948, 8th edition), 44.

2. Raymond E. Brown, SS, *The Gospel according to John, I–XII*, 50.

3. Marie-Joseph Lagrange, *Evangile selon saint Matthieu*, 49.

4. Lagrange, *Evangile selon saint Matthieu*, 56.

5. Lagrange, *Evangile selon saint Matthieu*, 57.

6. Marie-Joseph Lagrange, *Evangile selon saint Marc* (Paris: Gabalda, 1947), 2.

7. Lagrange, *Evangile selon saint Matthieu*, 6.

8. Hans Urs von Balthasar, *The Glory of the Lord: A Theological Aesthetics. VII: The New Covenant* (Edinburgh: T. and T. Clark, 1989), 41.

9. Hans Urs von Balthasar, *The Glory of the Lord*, 56.

10. Hans-Jochen Jaschke, *Der Heilige Geist im Bekenntnis der Kirche: Eine Studie zur Pneumatologie des Irenäus von Lyon im Ausgang vom altchristlichen Glaubensbekenntnis* (Münster: Aschendorff, 1976), 213, with reference to Irenaeus, *Against the Heresies*, III. 9, 3.

11. Hans-Jochen Jaschke, *Der Heilige Geist im Bekenntnis der Kirche*, 214.

12. Ildefonsus Schuster, *The Sacramentary* (London: Burns, Oates and Washbourne, 1924), I., 400.

13. Hans-Jochen Jaschke, *Der Heilige Geist im Bekenntnis der Kirche*, 210, with reference to Irenaeus, *Against the Heresies*, III, 17, 1 who points out that the Scriptures know nothing of a higher Redeemer coming down at the Baptism.

14. Ildefonsus Schuster, *The Sacramentary*, I., 400.

15. Schuster, *The Sacramentary*, 400, 401.

16. Schuster, *The Sacramentary*, 401.

17. Schuster, *The Sacramentary*, 401.

18. Irénée-Henri Dalmais, Pierre Jounel, Aimé Georges Martimort, *The Church at Prayer, An Introduction to the Liturgy, IV. The Liturgy and Time* (London: Chapman, 1986), 87.

19. Dalmais et al., *The Church at Prayer*, 88.

20. So we read at the beginning of *Summa theologiae,* IIIa., q. 39, which deals with this topic.

21. Ambrose, *Commentary on St. Luke's Gospel*, II (on Luke 3:21).

22. Pseudo-Chrysostom, *Incomplete Commentary on St. Matthew's Gospel*, IV (on Matthew 3:13).

23. Gregory Nazianzen, *Oration* 39.

24. Compare Thomas Aquinas, *Summa theologiae*, IIIa., q. 39, a. 6, ad iii.

25. Aquinas, IIIa., q. 39, a. 8, corpus.

26. Mother Mary and Archimandrite Kallistos Ware (tr.), *The Festal Menaion*, 58.

27. Sergius Bulgakov, *Churchly Joy: Orthodox Devotions for the Church Year* (Grand Rapids, MI: Eerdmans, 2008), 57–58.

28. Vladimir Lossky and Leonid Ouspensky, *The Meaning of Icons* (Crestwood, NY: St Vladimir's Seminary Press, 1982), 164, with a citation of John Damascene, *On the Orthodox Faith* III. 16.

29. Vladimir Lossky and Leonid Ouspensky, *The Meaning of Icons*, 165.

Chapter Eight

Transfiguration

Christ's Transfiguration follows on the Confession of Peter at Caesarea Philippi, and in the Synoptic Gospels these two interrelated events form a turning point in the entire narrative, a prelude to the climactic events of the story.

That Transfiguration prelude might better be called an overture. Through these inter-actions it sounds the key themes of the Paschal Mystery, which are the sacrificial Death and glorious Exaltation of the Incarnate Word. As, moreover, an event in its own right, the Transfiguration is also, like the Baptism, a theophany, a manifestation of the Holy Trinity who alone is God. As such it enables the Paschal Mystery to be set in the only context where that Mystery gains its full sense, namely, in the content of the being and action of the Triune God. That great biblical theologian Michael Ramsey went so far as to call the Transfiguration not just a "gateway to the saving events of the Gospel" but "a mirror in which the Christian mystery is seen in its unity."[1]

> Here we perceive that the living and the dead are one, that the old covenant and the new are inseparable, that the Cross and the glory are of one, that the age to come is already here, that our human nature has a destiny of glory, that in Christ the final word is uttered and in Him alone the Father is well pleased. Here the diverse elements in the theology of the New Testament meet.[2]

The Gospels do not specify on which mountain the Transfiguration took place. But that careful early fourth-century Church historian Eusebius, who was living on the Palestine coast, considered two candidates plausible. These were Mount Hermon, in the north of Galilee, or Mount Thabor at its center. Later in the century, St. Cyril of Jerusalem opted decisively for the second, and Cyril has usually been followed by Church writers ever since. But probably Mount Hermon has the better claim. As Dom Bargil Pixner points out, the historian Josephus gives the impression Thabor was populated at the time, and it had a Hasmonaean fortress on its summit. This would have been rather in the way. By contrast, Hermon was "generally considered in the local tradition as a holy mountain. The Hebrew word "Hermon" can be translated as "The Mountain Set Apart."[3] Hermon had an inherited appropriateness for the Transfiguration event. The identification of the site of the event is not nearly so important as grasping its meaning.

Any holy mountain in Israel would naturally remind Jews of Sinai, and, to be sure, the figure of Moses in this supernatural scene makes that reminiscence unavoidable, and Moses here contributes significantly to the Transfiguration's message. "When Moses ascended the mountain to be embraced by the Shekinah cloud he was publicly validated before all Israel as the supreme mediator of God's authoritative Torah. On his descent from the mountain, his radiant and transfigured face inspired awe in the people."[4] As to Elijah, his "ascent on the Merkabah comes as the prophet's glorification after he has faithfully fulfilled his prophetic ministry. That ministry was so charismatically great that Judaic tradition afterwards hailed him as one of the very few immortalized men inhabiting the court of Yahweh, enjoying even now the vision of the divine light."[5] In the simplest terms, the message concerns Jesus's glory—symbolized by the cloud of the divine Presence—which, as the beloved Son of the Father, is his by right. His glory exceeds, indeed belongs to a different order than that of even his greatest predecessors in Israel. The "great emphasis Mark puts on the sudden disappearance of Elijah and Moses, doubly stressed by the "saw no one any more" and the "but Jesus alone" [Mark 9:8], argues that for him the prophets have served their purpose, and so the stage is now cleared once again so that full attention may be given to reflecting on the status of Jesus who *alone* has received the title Son of God from the voice of Yahweh."[6] But the Messiah will only enter upon his glory definitively, as man, by the road of suffering and humiliation.

What of the Fathers? In the words of one contemporary scholar, "The Patristic interpretation of the Transfiguration of Jesus gives us the Fathers at their very best."[7] In a sermon on this mystery, St. Leo declared,

> The principal object of the transfiguration was to remove from the hearts of the disciples the scandal of the cross. The humiliation of a Passion willingly accepted would no longer trouble their faith, after the transcendence of the hidden mystery of the Son of God had been revealed.[8]

For Leo, the three witnesses on Thabor (let us, with the fifth-century pope, call it so) represent the entire Church. The Father's voice was meant not just for the apostles but for all later disciples, confirming their faith, foreshadowing their adoption as sons (in the beloved Son), and promising (implicitly) that they will be co-heirs with Christ to glory. "The Transfiguration reveals in Christ, the head of the mystical body, the transformation that the body as a whole is destined to receive."[9] At this date, however, the feast itself was not celebrated at Rome. It emerged in the Syrian Christian milieu, perhaps with the dedication of a church on Mount Thabor as spur.[10] From Syria it spread to Byzantium and ultimately to the West.

The Byzantine Church has regarded it with especial love. On the Vigil of the Transfiguration the Greek Church invites its faithful:

> Today Christ on Mount Thabor has changed the darkened nature of Adam, and filling it with brightness He has made it godlike. Shining forth with the light of the virtues, let us set foot on the holy mountain that we may gaze upon the divine Transfiguration of the Lord. The sun which makes the earth bright sets once more; but Christ has shone as lightning with glory upon the mountain and has filled the earth with light.[11]

It is a text that mirrors St. John Damascene's Trinitarian interpretation of the Transfiguration mystery: "The voice of the Father came from the cloud of the Spirit: This is my beloved Son. This is He who Is."[12] Ramsey, in his biblical theology, itself, surely, patristically inspired, had highlighted the prevision, in the Transfiguration, of the Paschal Mystery. At Mattins of the feast in the Byzantine rite, the kontakion agrees: "Thou wast transfigured upon the mountain, and Thy disciples beheld thy glory, O Christ our God, as far as they were able so to do: that when they saw Thee crucified, they might know that Thy suffering was voluntary, and might proclaim unto the world that Thou art truly the Brightness of the Father.[13] " It is the pure doctrine of Leo though, no doubt, independently arrived at.

That Liturgy also regards the Transfiguration as a summary of the whole doctrine of man's divinization by the glory of Christ. From as early as Athanasius the Great, the Greek Fathers had understood the purpose of the Incarnation of the Logos as the elevation of human nature to a better ontological condition. St. Andrew of Crete links this specifically to the Transfiguration mystery, telling the faithful, "Today we celebrate this feast, the deification of our nature, its transformation to a better condition, its rapture and ascent from natural realities to those which are above nature."[14] But, as the *kontakion* cited shows, the Byzantine Church does not forget the Passion and Death. A praise of the Cross is sung daily between the Transfiguration festival on August 6 and the feast of the Triumph of the Cross on September 14, so as to underline precisely this connection.

In the texts of the Transfiguration festival, and the theological comments of writers in both West and East, special importance is attached to the light that Christ radiates when he is transfigured before his disciples and shows them his divine nature, united without confusion with his human nature, for the first time. "Light was that Godhead which was shown on the mountain to the disciples, too strong for their eyes."[15] In the brilliance that momentarily blinds the disciples and, in the words of the Greek Liturgy again, makes them "fall with their faces to the ground," they are in fact "enlightened by the light of the Trinity, brighter than the sun, they see the glory of Christ."[16] In their turn, the disciples prefigure the transformation of all humanity by the Trinity's action in Christ. The true Beauty flows out from divine being to transform those who have purified their minds and are thus able to see it. That is how the fourteenth-century theologian of the Uncreated Light, St. Gregory Palamas—here followed by the great majority of Orthodox theologians of the modern period—typically puts it.

St. Thomas resembles the Byzantines (and Leo) in that his reflections on the Transfiguration are also a trailer for the Paschal Mystery. At the Transfiguration, what the Lord spoke about with the preternatural figures—representatives of the Law and the Prophets—was his coming Passion, and in the admonition that followed, he warned his disciples not to speak of what they had seen and heard until his Resurrection. The Transfiguration mystery is to strengthen the disciples to bear the Passion, which means not just their share in sufferings but that test of their faith which was their Master's terrible manner of dying. For their encouragement, the Christ of the Transfiguration episode gave those who were to follow in the footsteps of his Passion a bodily glimpse of the splendor that was properly his to bestow. As Thomas sums it up, "The splendour of our future glory was foreshadowed in the Transfiguration."[17] He writes "*our* future glory" since just as the Baptism of Christ announced the first regeneration, when by the rites of Baptism administered by the Church human beings start to live the life of sanctifying grace, so the Transfiguration of Christ announces their second regeneration, when "in the resurrection [of the body] he will give his elect the splendor of glory and refreshment from every evil."[18] Here Aquinas sees the Transfiguration as eschatological anticipation, though he does not relate it explicitly to the Parousia, as several of the Greek Fathers do, notably Cyril of Alexandria, for whom the glory revealed on Thabor anticipates the radiance the returning Lord will have at his second Advent.[19] Thomas's discussion brings him instead to the topic of Christ's *exitus*, his "exit" from this world with its super-abundant consequences for human salvation. Of course even the Parousia is an entailment of that "exit."

It is sometimes asked why when the Savior had three times predicted his Passion and Resurrection, once in the unforgettable context of the Transfiguration event, the disciples somehow could not grasp what he was saying. Balthasarians offer an explanation: "The eschatology and apocalyptic of the tradition in which [the disciples] had been brought up offered no help. It looked forward to the general resurrection at the end of history but knew nothing of an anticipated or proleptic resurrection. In the resurrection of Jesus, says Balthasar, the eschatology of the Old Testament "itself dies and rises again; it is fulfilled by being shattered."[20]

Bulgakov would look back to the Baptism, where the Father's "voice of filiation" ("This is my Beloved Son") was also heard (compare Matthew 17:5 with Matthew 3:14) and forward to the Passion—where in St. John's Gospel (John 12:28), the Father's voice speaks of Christ's coming glorification.

> The Father crowns with glory the Son's sacrificial will and confirms it as if with a new filiation. The Lord's Transfiguration, understood in this sense, is the spiritually pre-accomplished self-sacrifice of the Son, in accordance with the Father's will. It is the filial "Thy will be done."[21]

What of the icons of this feast? On the icons, the portrait of Christ high on the mountain recalls the image of Christ crucified lifted high on the Cross. Artists in the Byzantine tradition tend to present the mountain as three rocky peaks, for they are modeling their painting on the iconography of Mount Sinai. There are in fact three "mounts" involved here: Sinai, Thabor (which we shall take to stand for Hermon), and Golgotha. Thabor renews not only the inaugural New Testament theophany of the Baptism but the chief Old Testament theophany of Sinai. The Lord revealed himself to Moses on that mountain, and there too he drew close to Elijah, hidden in his cave on "Horeb," Sinai's alternative name. Thabor also points ahead to Golgotha, to Mount Calvary, which will be the summit—in every sense!—of the saving divine activity vis-à-vis the human race.

On the icons of the Transfiguration, the apostles are depicted in a variety of postures. But from the eleventh century on, the positions of Peter and John at least tend to remain the same, one kneeling, the other falling. By the fourteenth century the drama intensifies, with all three disciples falling precipitately: Peter and John onto their knees, James on his back, protecting his eyes with a hand. This serves, so it is suggested, to underline the "uncreated" character of the light issuing from the figure of Christ. This light was no ordinary physical light. That conviction was the message of the Hesychast controversy to which the figure of Palamas is key. Three rays pointing down at the apostles signalize the Trinitarian character of the divine action. Meanwhile Christ himself, in shining white raiment, stands on the mountain top with, to his right, Moses holding the book of the Decalogue, and to his left an elderly Elijah, portrayed with the long hair of an Eastern ascetic. Iconographers have sometimes stressed the eschatological implications of the central figures, with Moses representing Israel's dead and Elijah, who, in the Books of the Kings, did not die but was taken to heaven in a chariot, representing the living. Thus in a post-medieval Serbian icon, an angel is shown drawing Moses from the tomb while another brings Elijah out from a cloud, to be co-present on the mountain with the Savior. The Russian dogmatician Vladimir Lossky liked this, for it "underlines the eschatological character of the Transfiguration. Christ appears as the Lord of the quick and the dead, coming in the glory of the future age. The Transfiguration was 'an anticipation of His glorious Second Coming,' says St. Basil, the moment which opened a perspective of eternity in time."[22]

NOTES

1. Arthur Michael Ramsey, *The Glory of God and the Transfiguration of Christ* (London: Darton, Longman and Todd, 1967 [1949]), 144.

2. Ramsey, *The Glory of God*, 144.

3. Bargil Pixner, O.S.B., *W ith Jesus through Galilee according to the Fifth Gospel* (Rosh Pina: Corazin Publishing, 1992), 98.

4. John Anthony McGuckin, *The Transfiguration of Christ in Scripture and Tradition* (Lewiston, NY: Edwin Mellen Press, 1987), 13.

5. McGuckin, *The Transfiguration of Christ*, 16. Though Deuteronomy stated Moses died on Mount Nebo (Deuteronomy 34:5), the account given was "sufficiently mysterious to allow for legendary development." McGuckin, *The Transfiguration of Christ*, 46.

6. McGuckin, *The Transfiguration of Christ*, 70.

7. McGuckin, *The Transfiguration of Christ*, 99.

8. Leo, *Sermon* 51.

9. J. Mark Armitage, *A Twofold Solidarity* (Strathfield, NSW: St Paul's Publications, 2005), 99.

10. Irénée-Henri Dalmais, Pierre Jounel, and Aimé Georges Martimort, *The Church at Prayer, An Introduction to the Liturgy, IV: The Liturgy and Time* (Paris: Editions du Cerf, 2012), 97.

11. Mother Mary and Archimandrite Kallistos Ware (tr.), *The Festal Menaion*, 469.

12. John of Damascus, *On the Transfiguration*, 16.

13. Mother Mary and Archimandrite Kallistos Ware (tr.), *The Festal Menaion*, 489.

14. Andrew of Crete, *Festal Homily*, 1.

15. Gregory Nazianzen, *Oration* 40, 6.

16. Arthur Michael Ramsey, *The Glory of God and the Transfiguration of Christ*, 144.

17. Thomas Aquinas, *Summa theologiae*, IIIa., q. 45, a. 4, corpus.

18. Aquinas, IIIa., q. 45, a. 1, ad ii.

19. Cyril of Alexandria, *Homily* 9.

20. John Saward, *The Mysteries of March*, 137.

21. Sergius Bulgakov, *Churchly Joy: Orthodox Devotions for the Church Year* (Grand Rapids, MI: Eerdmans, 2008), op., cit., 139–140.

22. Vladimir Lossky and Leonid Ouspensky, *The Meaning of Icons* (Crestwood, NY: St Vladimir's Seminary Press, 1982), 212, with an internal citation of Basil's Homily on Psalm 44.

Chapter Nine

Passion and Death

Good Friday has a preamble. Not the least extraordinary thing about Passion Week is the prophecy recorded of the Jewish High Priest in St. John's Gospel to the effect that—speaking ironically, in defense of an act of judicial murder—a great multitude would benefit from this one man's death (John 11:52). In John's interpretation of this singular prophecy, Jesus was going to die so that the dispersed children of God might become one with the Israelite nation at its true heart. This is pertinent to the Church of the Holy Eucharist, the Eucharist instituted on the eve of Good Friday.

> It is scarcely accidental that John's description of redeemed Jews and Gentiles gathered into one echoes the terminology of the eucharistically oriented multiplication of the loaves (John 6:13) where the fragments are *gathered together.*[1]

So much was already realized by the author of that ancient Christian treatise the *Didache*, or "Teaching of the Twelve Apostles," which echoes both the Multiplication of the Loaves and this sacerdotal hitting on the truth.[2] The evangelist John's interpretation of the "prophecy" takes for granted the redemptive nature of Jesus's death. This was no innovation on his part, any more than (as has sometimes been alleged), it was innovatory on the part of Paul, except, so far as the latter is concerned, in one regard. As the American exegete Larry Hurtado explains,

> Paul's own contribution was not to coin the idea that Jesus' death and resurrection were redemptive, nor to make this idea central to early Christian beliefs. The tradition that Paul cites explicitly shows that this idea had long been a key feature of circles of believers that appear to take us back to the Jerusalem church. But in Jewish Christian usage, the view of Jesus' death as redemptive had served mainly Christological concerns, giving a rationale for the death of

God's messiah. Paul's innovation lay in contending that this traditional view of Christ's death and resurrection also gave a rationale for the programmatic salvation of Gentiles without their observance of Torah, an aim which he believed himself called to obtain through his Gentile mission.[3]

The redemptive deed of the Lord would be equally pertinent to the *Ecclesia ex Circumcisione* and to the *Ecclesia ex Gentibus*—and on the same terms.

On the day before Good Friday, in the Rome of the patristic age, a community classically composed from the outset of Jewish and Gentile converts, three Masses were customarily celebrated. In the first place, there was a Mass for the reconciliation of the penitents at the completion of their canonical penance. With the introduction of private Confession and Absolution, this eventually fell into desuetude, but cathedrals (and other churches) following Roman usage replaced it with the choral office of *Tenebrae*. In that office the recital of the Lamentations of Jeremiah continues the same expression of the repentance and plea for forgiveness of Israel/Church. Secondly, there was a Mass for the consecration of the oils to be used for the initiation of new Christians—and new priests and bishops to continue the life of the Church. Thirdly, there was the Mass of the *Coena Domini*, the Lord's Supper itself. This trio of celebrations depended on the redemptive act begun this day, the first of the *Triduum*. Here, therefore, the Supper-Mass, with its special relation to that act, must be regarded as preeminent.

On the eve of Good Friday, the redemptive Sacrifice the Messiah was to offer "for the multitude" was, in advance, encompassed through the institution of its sign. That day is the birthday of the Mass, with its intimate relation to the sacrifice of Christ—a relation of identity the sixteenth century Council of Trent will call it, meaning *sacramental* identity of course, since the Mass takes place in the realm of signs. Using a distinction made famous by the twentieth-century Scholastic theologian, Maurice de la Taille: at the Supper, the Servant-Messiah was *oblandus*, "to be offered," whereas on the Cross, he was *oblatus*, "actually offered." But the act of self-oblation was morally, and in its sign dimension, one and the same. Jesus acts as high priest of his own sacrificial death thanks to the way that, at the Supper, he offers up his life ritually. Supper and Cross will form a single sacrifice, for the "the will, the love, the *devotio*" is the same in both.[4] Though the entire series of actions from the Garden of Gethsemane to the Cross is evidence for the Lord's self-surrender to the Passion, it was well that the sacrificial nature of his coming death as an act of adoration and expiation were "plainly evident as a sign."[5]

It is obvious how this mystery of Christ becomes our mystery. It is through the kind of sacramental life made possible by the Holy Eucharist instituted on this day. The Mass instituted on the eve of Good Friday is a sacrifice that ends in a sacred meal. Partaking of the sacrificial banquet signifies both glory—sharing in the divine gifts of heaven in time to come, the Messianic banquet—and grace, spiritual union with God through Christ here and now, which includes union with him in his ecclesial members. That is perfectly summed up in the Eucharistic antiphon of St. Thomas Aquinas: "O sacred banquet, in which Christ is received, the memory of his Passion is renewed, the mind is filled with grace, and a pledge of future glory is given us." One Orthodox and one Anglican theologian may be brought now to the witness stand. Father Alexander Schmemann, erstwhile Dean of St. Vladimir's Seminary in New York, noted in this context the significance of St. John's statement that on the night before Christ suffered he loved his disciples "to the end" (John 13: 1).

> In the eucharistic experience and in the gospels the last supper is the end (*telos*), i.e. the completion, the crowning, the fulfillment of Christ's love, which constitutes the essence of all of his ministry, preaching, miracles, and through which he now gives himself up as love itself. From the opening words, "I have earnestly desired to eat this passover with you" (Luke 22: 15) to the exit to the garden of Gethsamene, everything at the last supper—the washing of the feet, the distribution to the disciples of the bread and the cup, the last discourse—is not only concerned with love but is *Love itself*. And thus the last supper is the *telos*, the completion, the fulfillment of the *end*, for it is the manifestation of that kingdom of love, for the sake of which the world was created.[6]

And Schmemann continues:

> If in the services of Holy Thursday, the day of the express commemoration of the last supper, joy is all the time laced with sadness, if the Church again and again recalls not only the light but also the darkness overshadowing it, it is because, in the double exits of Judas and Christ from that light into that darkness, she sees and knows the beginning of the cross as the mystery of sin and the mystery of victory over it.[7]

Archbishop Michael Ramsey of Canterbury would apply the term "glory" throughout, "darkness" and the "beginning of the cross" notwithstanding. In his handling of the loaf and the cup, the Savior at the Supper dedicates himself for a sacrificial death, glorifying the Father while consecrating himself for the disciples. The glory he gives them, in the Fourth Gospel's High Priestly Prayer, is nothing other than their feeding upon his sacrificially surrendered life. And that is why for St. Paul, writing to the Corinthians, the Eucharistic rite can be said to show forth Christ's death in all its glory, and unite "those who partake with the glory of Christ as He now is—risen, ascended and glorifying the Father."[8]

But we have not yet explored for its own sake the Trinitarian dimension of the relation between the institution of the Holy Eucharist and the Passion and Death. Here Balthasar's theology is rich.

The Eucharist has its presupposition in the life of the Trinity. In the inner life of the Godhead, the divine essence which the Son eternally receives from the Father he offers back to him in gratitude, in love, in the Holy Trinity. The Son is thanksgiving in his very person, "the Father's substantial Eucharist." Of course, since Jesus is true man as well as true God, he is not Eucharist in this Trinitarian sense alone. His eternal thankful return of his divinity to the Father is incarnated in the surrender of his human body and soul, in the Holy Spirit, to the Father. As God from eternity, and man from the Virgin's womb, the Son's love is grateful and self-giving. In his divinity, with regard to the generating Father, he is Eucharist in the sense of eternal gratitude. In his humanity, with regard to his brethren he is Eucharist in the sense of a love that wants to distribute itself, a body ready to be broken, blood to be poured out, a heart to be wounded. And the two movements are one. In offering his body for us, in giving his body to us, the thankful Son fulfils his Father's will that we be drawn into the life of the Blessed Trinity. "As the living Father sent me, and I live because of the Father, so he who eats me will live because of me" (John 6:57).[9]

So much for what I have called the "preamble." But the Passion and Death could not remain only in the will, or on the Supper board. On Good Friday, the ritual outpouring of wine and breaking of bread was realized in bloody flux and maceration of the flesh. At Passover this was already so for the animal creation. The blood and water of beasts already flowed out from the altar of the Temple, the sole place where sacrificial worship could lawfully be carried out. But now a new Sacrifice is offered. The opening of Jesus's side in the nineteenth chapter of St. John's Passion narrative accords with this: the Temple, site of the myriad sacrifices of beasts, is replaced by the sacrificial body of the Lord, from which blood and water also flow. What began in the Upper Room is completed, the Temple's purpose fulfilled, Jesus's own Temple identity revealed. Gustaf Dalman commented on the cry "It is finished" in the Fourth Gospel (John 19:30), "The last Word from the Cross expresses the fact that this life-work had been brought to a successful close; a superhuman task had been put upon Him, now, since it has been accomplished, He can go back to Him who had sent Him."[10]

What of the Fathers of the Church on this stupendous event? They understand it as the climactic event of the movement of descent the Word undertook in the Incarnation. Thus for Gregory Nazianzen, "The Cross of Jesus Christ is . . . the culmination and fulfillment of the *oikonomia* of the Incarnation. It is the prime instrument of salvation. Gregory sees made manifest on the Cross of Calvary the deeper meaning of the condescension and self-emptying of the Son of God, and of his recapitulation of the entire created order."[11] The patrologist Donald Winslow sums up Gregory's teaching on the mystery of the Passion and Death when he writes,

God *comes down*—all the way down—to the lowest level of our fallen condition, namely death. God *empties himself* of his glory and humbles himself before the altar of divine sacrificial love. And God *resumes in himself* the misdirected pilgrimage of the First Adam, thereby obliterating on the Tree of the Cross the consequences of the violation of the Tree of Knowledge so that we might once more partake of the Tree of Life.[12]

Evidently, there is here a combination of suffering and triumph. Though the latter, coming at the end of this trio of motifs, rightly indicates the goal and outcome of the rest, it remains the case that the biblical image Gregory uses most frequently for the Cross is that of sacrifice.[13] From what is perhaps the earliest patristic theology of the Paschal events that we have, Melito of Sardis *On the Pasch*, we see how that "combination" is the leitmotiv of the patristic celebration of those events. "Overall [*Peri Pascha*] is a commemoration of the sufferings and triumph of the now exalted saviour-lamb."[14] "The true doctrine of atonement," wrote Michael Ramsey, in an excellent summary of the mind of the patristic age, "is the doctrine of *Christus Victor*: but it includes (what some of its exponents forget) expiation as the price and the means of victory."[15] Rightly, patrologists have criticized the Swedish Lutheran bishop Gustaf Aulén for his influential reduction of patristic soteriology to a single *Christus victor* "model"—to the detriment, not to say complete exclusion, of other themes available to a patristic synthesis. His fellow-Swede Lars Koen, writing to this effect,[16] cites tellingly some words of Leonard Hodgson, sometime canon professor at Christ Church, Oxford: "Bishop Aulén succumbs to the besetting temptation of transactionists, the temptation so to emphasize the godhead of the Redeemer as to reduce the manhood of Christ to a passive, indeed to a docetic role."[17]

In St. Leo, by contrast, the two "forms" of Christ, the "glory" of the divine form and the "degradation" (*contumelia*) of the human form are held together in the unity of his person, on the Cross as everywhere else. He could not redeem us unless he represented us in what we are—fearful, suffering, and under the shadow of permanent death, just as, equally, he could not redeem us were he not endowed with all the Father has, enabling him to defeat these powers and show they are not to be feared. These two conditions do not, however, suffice for an understanding of the Atonement unless we add that, in all he suffered and did in his Passion and Death, he acted meritoriously to win for us our reward. Christ "prepares a *beatus transitus* for the faithful by accepting the cross in such a way as to merit the glorification of his flesh (the theology of Philippians 2:5-11), thereby establishing the Paschal mystery as a *sacramentum* which empowers the *beatus transitus* and as an *exemplum* which models it."[18]

This is the doctrine not only of St. Paul but also of St. John.

[T]he *Christus Victor* doctrine does not stand alone: it includes, in the Fourth Gospel, the doctrine of a godward offering whereby sin is expiated . . . Hence in the story of the Passion the imagery of the victorious king who reigns from the tree is blended with the imagery of the sacrificial victim who expiates sin and brings communion between God and man, slain as he is at the Passover time (John 19:14) and slain as a peace-offering without the breaking of a bone (John 19: 36). The victory and the expiation are inseparable and the *doxa* [glory] expresses this.[19]

There is no *Christus victor* without the *Christus crucifixus*, no victory without sacrifice, in whose absence the glory, deprived of its dimension of self-giving, cannot properly be thought.

As to Thomas Aquinas, when he comes to speak of the efficacy of the Passion of Christ he takes the opportunity to refresh his readers' memory of the principles he set out earlier in the "Third Part" of the *Summa theologiae*, and especially the notion of the "capital grace" of Christ, his grace as Head of his mystical Body. As Thomas reminds them, "Christ was given grace not only as an individual but in so far as he is head of the Church, so that grace might pour out from him upon his members."[20] And he draws the appropriate inference, " Thus there is the same relation between Christ's deeds for himself and his members, as there is between what another man does in the state of grace and himself."[21] In his Passion, then, Christ merited not just salvation for himself—in fact he needed none, except for the glorification of his own body—but for others. Indeed, his Passion meant atonement that was "not only sufficient but superabundant" for the sins of the entire world.[22]

In this work of atonement, his flesh became the "perfect sacrifice," owing to the quality of the love with which it was offered.[23] Throughout this act of redemption it was, says Thomas, Christ in his humanity who was the "immediate Redeemer" of men, though the primal Cause of their redemption was the entire divine Trinity who "inspired" the human mind and will of the Redeemer to act and suffer as he did.[24] With Jesus's humanity working as the instrument of his divinity, and doing so through the action of freely submitting to the death of the Cross, the Passion of Christ accomplished humankind's salvation as its efficient if secondary cause.[25] With the Godhead joined to his humanity the efficacy of what Christ does in his human activity can be inexhaustible. This efficacy works for others, adds Thomas, through *contactus spiritualis*, "spiritual contact," brought about by "faith and the sacraments of faith."[26] It is by faith and the sacraments of faith that the life of the Mystical Body, the Church, is constituted and unfolds. So the mystery of the Lord's suffering and Death becomes the mystery of Christians. It becomes the source of their forgiveness, the means of their rescue from thralldom to evil and liability to penalty for misdeeds. And it does so "insofar as we are incorporated into him as members into the Head."[27] More positively still, the Passion is the mystery of Christians because it "opens for us the gate to heaven," even though it is only by Christ's Ascension (yet to be dealt with) that Christ leads us "into the possession of the heavenly kingdom."[28]

The Passion also sublimely exemplifies a maxim Thomas took, via Peter Lombard, from the patristic monastic founder Cassiodorus: *Christi actio fuit nostra instructio*, "Christ's action was our instruction."[29]

There is not a single example of virtue that the Cross

> does not give us. Do you seek an example of charity? "There is no greater love than to give up one's life for those we love." And Christ did it on the Cross. . . . Are you looking for an example of patience? The most perfect patience is found on the Cross. . . . An example of humility? Look upon the Crucified One. An example of obedience? Follow him who made himself obedient to the Father even unto death. . . . An example of scorn for earthly things? Walk after him who is King of Kings and Lord of Lords, in whom are found all the treasures of wisdom and who, nonetheless, appears naked on the Cross, an object of mockery, spit upon, beaten, crowned with thorns, offered gall and vinegar, put to death.[30]

Hans Urs von Balthasar's theology of Good Friday, much indebted to the mystic and lay theologian Adrienne von Speyr, embodies the theme of combined sadness and joy already accentuated by Schmemann on the Liturgy of Holy Thursday and by Ramsey on the Pasch of the Lord as a whole. In his *Theo-drama*, Balthasar wrote,

> When on the Cross, he redeems the world in order to complete the Father's joy, he does so "in the joy of the Father, but also in his own joy of giving the Father a gift. Yet in the midst of this joy there lies all the suffering of the Cross, which is not thereby lessened. 'If it be possible, let this cup pass from me': these are words of fear that, on the Cross, turn into words expressing his forsakenness. Nonetheless the whole darkness of suffering—even though it is the greatest suffering that ever was—is embraced, as it were, in the encompassing joy." For his part the Father "cannot give any answer, because he desires to give the Son perfect joy, namely the joy of having died for him in the experience of forsakenness." It is easy for us to forget that a Divine Person, even in the Incarnation and in the vicissitudes of his human "I," is nevertheless pure relation and that God's blessedness consists in his *being* self-surrender. When the Son accepts dying in the agony of God-forsakenness, it is for him (and the other Divine Persons) not only an "external work" undertaken out of absolute love and joy but also the expression of his very own, his very specific life.[31]

Ramsey had spoken of the Lord's journey to the Father as also a journey "deeper and deeper into humanity with its sin, its sorrow, and its death. . . . Towards heaven, towards the world's darkness: these were two facets of the one journey, the one Christ."[32]

Bulgakov wrote,

His final impoverishment for our sake is His enthronement, and the way to Golgotha is the way to victory.[33]

The literally crucial importance of this festival is shown in the uniquely rich ways in which it has been depicted in the arts of the Church.[34] Gems engraved with the motif of Christ on the Cross exist from the second and third centuries, while the British Museum has quite an elaborately composed Crucifixion scene in ivory that dates from the fifth century.

The early Syrian type of representation shows Christ alive with open eyes, robed, holding himself erect—as in the sixth-century Rabbula Gospels. This way of depicting the Crucified persisted for a long time in the West. It is the Christ of St. John's Gospel reigning from the tree, impassive and triumphant, and sometimes adorned with the ornaments befitting a King and High Priest. It was not possible for death to be held by him as St. Peter explains in the Jerusalem sermon in the Acts of the Apostles (2:24). But from the eleventh century onward, the Byzantine church developed a more obviously human rendering, showing Christ naked except for a loin cloth, and obviously dead, with closed eyes.[35] This scandalized the Latin legates who visited Constantinople in the 1050s to remonstrate with the patriarch over his shortcomings. Long before the realistic cult of the humanity took root in the West, the Byzantines saw the need to show more fully the *kenosis*—and this must be carefully distinguished from the desire simply to have a more naturalistic Christ. A theological point of great importance is being made. Unless there is emphasis on the lengths to which the voluntary humiliation went, the Easter triumph cannot be given its full value. The Byzantine polymath Michael Psellus, writing in the eleventh century, ascribes to the iconographer the almost impossible task of reconciling the contradiction between death and life in the Crucified. He must be shown breathing out his last breath, but with the beauty and form of someone fully animated.[36] Otherwise the Pasch as such cannot be depicted.

Early portrayal drew in elements from the Passion narratives in the canonical Gospels, especially the holy women (whom iconographers place behind Mary), the centurion who cried out in salutation of Christ in St. Mark, and accompanying soldiers (placed behind the Beloved Disciple). Later, elements were added from outside the Gospels in an attempt to indicate the full historical and indeed cosmic scope of the event. One thinks here of the underground cavern shown open so as to reveal the skull of Adam (a suggestion of the pan-historical nature of the event), and of the flying angels who home in on the Cross with an expression of wonder or sometimes grief (thus expressing the cosmic aspect of the mystery, since these are heavenly Powers). In Byzantine iconography, the blood running from Christ's feet flows onto Adam's skull. This was a Hebrew tradition reported by Origen and taken up in the third century by St. Epiphanius in his "On the Passion and

Cross of the Lord." Athanasius in the East, Ambrose in the West, accepted it at face value. Whether the proto-parent was actually buried on Golgotha is hardly of importance compared with the subjacent theological affirmation, which a text from the Byzantine Liturgy puts magnificently.

> Lifted high upon the Cross, O Master, with Thyself Thou hast raised up Adam and the whole of fallen nature. Therefore, exalting Thine undefiled Cross, O Thou who lovest mankind, we ask Thee for Thy strength from above, crying: O God Most High, in Thy mercy save those who honour the sacred, light-giving and divine Exaltation of Thy Cross. [37]

In the icons and despite the encompassing angels the Cross is very clearly planted in earth. It is the new Tree that symbolizes Paradise reopened. In that fourteenth-century English masterpiece of illuminated manuscript, the Sherborne Missal, new leaves spring from dead wood when they are touched by the blood of Christ. This is the chthonic dimension, which is also, like the angels, cosmic.

The role of Mary must not be overlooked. In the icons, an atmosphere of quiet contemplation and deep silent prayer owes much to the attitude of the Mother of God to her crucified Son. The role of the Beloved Disciple is subordinate here, despite their symmetrical placing on either side of the Redeemer. Typically, John's posture—his look, which takes in both Christ and Mary, and his gesture of placing his hand on the side of his head as though thinking—leads to meditation on the relation of the Mother and the Son. By contrast, the position given the Mother of the Lord resembles the way she is shown in the *Deesis*, the Byzantine icon of intercession where the *Theotokos* and that other St. John, John the Baptist, flank Christ the *Pantokrator*.

> As there is no boldness in us because of the multitude of our sins, do thou, O Virgin Theotokos, intercede with the Son whom thou hast borne, for the entreaty of His Mother had great power to win the favour of the Master. Despise not, O all-honoured Lady, the prayers of sinners, for he who took upon Himself to suffer for our sake is merciful and strong to save. [38]

The Mother, though called upon to intercede for others, is no less grief stricken for herself at the Passion of her Son. A tenth-century drawing in the Ramsey Psalter shows her lifting the fold of her cloak to her face as a symbol of grief, while Anselm of Canterbury in his theologically highly wrought "Prayer to Christ" cannot believe her to have held back tears. [39]

The richness of the imagery, and its variety, testify to the "excess" of the moment of the Cross in a theological perspective. It is a "gift exceeding every debt" in the title of a sympathetic account of Anselm's theology of the Sacrifice, which, surprisingly, is by an Eastern Orthodox scholar, for the

Orthodox are not usually so generous to the Latin Scholastics (in Anselm's case, a "pre-" or "early" Scholastic divine).[40]

> As an entirely divine action, Christ's sacrifice merely draws creation back into the eternal motion of divine love for which it was fashioned. The violence that befalls Christ belongs to the order of justice, an order overcome by his sacrifice, which is one of peace.[41]

NOTES

1. Raymond E. Brown, S. S., *The Gospel according to John I–XII*, 443.

2. *Didache* 9. 4.

3. Larry W. Hurtado, *Lord Jesus Christ: Devotion to Jesus in Earliest Christianity* (Grand Rapids, MH, and Cambridge: Eerdmans, 2005), 133.

4. Michon M. Matthiesen, *Sacrifice as Gift: Eucharist, Grace and Contemplative Prayer in Maurice de la Taille* (Washington, DC: Catholic University of America Press, 2013), 25.

5. Maurice de la Taille, S. J., *Mysterium fidei: De augustissimo corporis et sanguinis Christi sacrificio et sacramento* (Paris: Beauchesne, 1921), I., 46.

6. Alexander Schmemann, *The Eucharist, Sacrament of the Kingdom* (Crestwood, NY: St. Vladimir''s Seminary Press, 1987), 200.

7. Schmemann, *The Eucharist*, 205.

8. Arthur Michael Ramsey, *The Glory of God and the Transfiguration of Christ* (London: Darton, Longman and Todd, 1967 [1949]), 98.

9. John Saward, *The Mysteries of March: Hans Urs von Balthasar on the Incarnation and Easter* (London: Collins, 1990), 88–89, with an internal citation of Hans Urs von Balthasar, *New Elucidations* (San Francisco: Ignatius, 1986), 115.

10. Gustaf Dalman, *Jesus-Jeshua: Studies in the Gospels* (New York: Macmillan, 1929), 218.

11. Donald F. Winslow, *The Dynamics of Salvation: A Study in Gregory of Nazianzus* (Cambridge, MA: Philadelphia Patristic Foundation, 1979), 99.

12. Winslow, *The Dynamics of Salvation*, 99.

13. Winslow, *The Dynamics of Salvation*, 102.

14. Alistair Stewart-Sykes, *The Lamb's High Feast: Melito, Peri Pacha, and the Quartodeciman Paschal Liturgy at Sardis* (Leiden: Brill, 1998), 206.

15. Arthur Michael Ramsey, *The Glory of God and the Transfiguration of Christ*, 76.

16. Lars Koen, *The Saving Passion: Incarnational and Soteriological Thought in Cyril of Alexandria's Commentary on the Gospel according to St. John* (Stockholm: Almqvist & Wiksell, 1991), 128–31.

17. Leonard Hodgson, *The Doctrine of the Atonement* (New York: Charles Scribner and Sons, 1951), 147.

18. J. Mark Armitage, *A Twofold Solidarity: Leo the Great's Theology of Redemption* (Strathfield, NSW: St Paul's Publications, 2005), 110.

19. Arthur Michael Ramsey, *The Glory of God and the Transfiguration of Christ*, 86–87.

20. Thomas Aquinas, *Summa theologiae*, IIIa., q. 48, a. 1.

21. Aquinas, *Summa theologiae*, IIIa., q. 48, a. 1.

22. Aquinas, *Summa theologiae*, IIIa., q. 48, a. 2, corpus.

23. Aquinas, *Summa theologiae*, IIIa., q. 48, a. 3.

24. Aquinas, *Summa theologiae*, IIIa., q. 48, a. 5, corpus

25. Aquinas, *Summa theologiae*, IIIa., q. 45, a. 6.

26. Aquinas, *Summa theologiae*, IIIa., q. 45, a. 6, ad ii.

27. Aquinas, *Summa theologiae*, IIIa., q. 49, a. 4, ad ii.

28. Aquinas, *Summa theologiae*, IIIa., q. 49, a. 5, ad iv.

29. Richard Schenk, O. P., "*Omnis Christ actio fuit nostra instructio*. The Deeds and Sayings of Jesus as revelation in the View of Thomas Aquinas," in Leo Elders, S. V. D. (ed.), *La doctrine de la Révélation divine* (Vatican City: Vatican Polyglot press, 1990), 103–31.

30. Thomas Aquinas, *Exposition of the Creed*, 4, with an internal citation of John 15:13.

31. Hans Urs von Balthasar, *Theo-Drama, Theological Dramatic Theory. V. The Last Act*, 255, citing Adrienne von Speyr, *Der Mensch vor Gott* (Einsiedeln: Johannes Verlag, 1966), 82.

32. Arthur Michael Ramsey, *Sacred and Secular* (London: Longmans, 1965), 76.

33. Sergius Bulgakov, *Churchly Joy: Orthodox Devotions for the Church Year* (Grand Rapids, MI: Eerdmans, 2008), 93.

34. As testifies Gertrud Schiller, *Iconography of Christian Art. 2. The Passion of Jesus Christ* (London: Lund Humphries, 1972), on which my account draws.

35. Note that there may be early anticipation—for instance, three ninth-century panels showing the Crucified with closed eyes have been discovered at Sinai; see Kurt Weitzmann, *The Monastery of Saint Catherine at Mount Sinai: The Icons. Volume I: From the Sixth to the Tenth Century* (Princeton: Princeton University Press, 1976), B 32/36/50.

36. See Hans Belting, *Likeness and Presence: A History of the Image before the Era of Art* (Chicago and London: University of Chicago Press, 1994), 271, for what the distinguished German art historian thinks is a twelfth-century example, also on Sinai.

37. Mother Mary and Archimandrite Kallistos Ware (tr.), *The Festal Menaion*, 131.

38. Mother Mary and Archimandrite Kallistos Ware, *The Lenten Triodion* (London: Faber and Faber, 1978), 579.

39. Sister Benedicta Ward, S. L. G. (tr.), *The Prayers and Meditations of St. Anselm* (London: Penguin, 1973), 96.

40. David Bentley Hart, "A Gift Exceeding Every Debt: An Eastern Orthodox Appreciation of Anselm's *Cur Deus homo*," *Pro Ecclesia* VII. 3 (1998), 333–49.

41. Hart, "A Gift Exceeding Every Debt," 348.

Chapter Ten

Descent into Hell

Beyond the Passion and Death, is there any more to say where mysteries of the humiliation are concerned? Despite the separation of Christ's body and soul, which is what rendered him a dead man, each of these component elements of his being, body, and soul, remained personally united to God the Word. In regard to Jesus's postmortem existence, the question of his "descent" to the realm of the dead, seen as the end point of the movement of humiliation, is well nigh unavoidable, even if it were not included, under the title "He descended into Hell," in the Apostles' Creed.

In St. Matthew's Gospel the Savior prophesies he will lie for three days "in the heart of the earth" (Matthew 12:40), a reference to a sojourn in the underworld of the dead. Elsewhere in the New Testament, the "Descent into Hell seems to be connected in some special way with the preaching of St. Peter."[1] In his Jerusalem address on the day of Pentecost in the Acts of the Apostles (Acts 2:31), Peter makes use of Psalm 15 to argue that King David, wearing a prophet's mantle, "foresaw that Christ's soul would not be abandoned to Hades, nor his flesh see corruption."[2] And in his First Letter, Peter writes on two occasions of the postmortem Savior preaching to the dead (First Peter 3:1–1a, and 4:6). The soul of Jesus, separated from its body but not from the Logos, spent time, then, in Sheol, the only afterlife human beings knew before the work of their redemption was complete.

A homily ascribed to St. Epiphanius of Salamis, now used in the Roman Rite for the Office of Readings of Holy Saturday, combines the notes of humiliation and triumph. "What is happening? Today there is a great silence over the earth, a great silence, and stillness, a great silence because the King sleeps; the earth was in terror and was still, because God slept in the flesh and raised up those who were sleeping from the ages. God died in the flesh, and the underworld has trembled."[3] Likewise at Mattins of Holy Saturday the Byzantine Church both laments and rejoices.

> All things above and all beneath the earth quaked with fear at Thy death, as they beheld Thee, O my Saviour, upon Thy throne on high and in the tomb below. For beyond our understanding Thou dost lie before our eyes, a corpse yet the very Source of Life. To fill all things with Thy glory, Thou hast gone down into the nethermost parts of the earth: for my person that is in Adam has not been hidden from Thee, but in Thy love for man Thou art buried in the tomb and dost restore me from corruption.[4]

In recent Roman Catholicism, the descent of Christ's soul into Hell has become rather a controversial topic, owing to its presentation by Balthasar as the last of the mysteries of Christ's humiliation, rather than the first of the mysteries of his exaltation. St. Thomas has at least a touch of Balthasar's perspective when he bases the fittingness of Christ's descent into Hell on how "he came to bear our punishment and to free us from it,"[5] citing the words of Isaiah, "he has borne our infirmities and carried our sorrows" (Isaiah 53:4). Here Holy Saturday is an appendage to Good Friday rather than a prelude to Easter Sunday. But Thomas's main stress lies elsewhere. The effects of Christ's descent brought glory to the holy men of the Old Testament, the hope of glory to those now in Purgatory, and confutation to the damned.[6]

For Aquinas, the Descent is not a mystery of Christ which can be a mystery of Christians if by this is meant a mystery to be shared by those alive today. A possible exception, not noted by Thomas, is the Christian mystic who may have a share in the mystery of Christ's Descent owing to his or her solidarity with the (negative) spiritual situation of others, insofar as such solidarity is made possible by the Communion of Saints.

The joy of the liberation of Adam is not, however, the whole story. Or, rather, the whole story needs dark tones for the radiant joy to be seen in its true colors. Balthasar wrote,

> The descent of Jesus into the reality of death that preceded Redemption is part of his humiliation, even though this ultimate humiliation, beyond which no other is possible, is already shot through with the light of Easter night, as is for St. John even the Cross itself. For this journey through Hades carries Redemption into it. This track through the trackless way makes an opening where before all had been completely closed. For this uttermost loneliness of death of him who has lost all connexion with the living, whose body lies fettered in its tomb and whose soul lets itself be bound with the bonds of the experience of Hades, introduces everything that is called communication and communion in the eternal sense. For this darkest of all dark nights of the soul sheds an eternal light where, without this vicarious night, there would have been only eternal darkness.[7]

It was Balthasar's conviction that the Byzantine East had missed out here on something the Latin West knew well: the "dark nights" spoken of by the Catholic mystics, notably in the Carmelite tradition if not only there. As he puts it, there can be such things as "descents into hell as a Christian grace, that is as an imitation of Christ."[8] It is not just a question of subjective purification, but of an objective following of Christ, and one that, by a process called by Paul the "completing" of "whatever is lacking to the sufferings of Christ" (Colossians 1:24), contributes to redemption, for it is undergone "in order that the darkness of the world might be turned into light."[9] The light cannot be seen in its full force unless the darkness is estimated at its true strength.

> If the atonement is supposed to heal the human situation, sin must be eradicated by God's identification with us precisely in our being separated from God. . . . The *descensus* of Holy Saturday is the depth dimension of the Cross itself.[10]

The entirety of Balthasar's theology of the Descent depends on the ability to show in what way the Passion, Death, and Descent *even in their negative meaning* can constitute an act of mutual love between Father and Son—and thus an action that takes place by the Holy Spirit. What Balthasar calls a change in modality of the relation between Father and Son, beginning on the Cross, is not the end of their love. On the contrary, it is its resilience under changed conditions. Balthasar speaks of the "soteriological modalization of the relationship between Father, Son and Spirit,"[11] whereby "separation" itself becomes a "mode of union."[12]

> We have to show . . . that the God-forsakenness of the Son during his Passion was just as much a mode of his profound bond with the Father in the Holy Spirit as his death was a mode of his life and his suffering a mode of his bliss.[13]

Balthasar's texts should not of course be taken Monophysitically. What Christ does, says, and is *translates* the divine being—it is *not identical* with that being, which itself is uncreated. Accordingly, Balthasar makes it plain that when Christ suffers God does not suffer, a verb which, with God as subject, he places in inverted commas. Yet "Christ's suffering, his God-forsakenness, his death and descent into hell is the revelation of a divine mystery, the language which God has chosen in order to render himself and his love intelligible to us."[14] And this in turn means that the "language" used has been anticipated (or we should not have an inkling of what it communicates) and also echoed (or it would not have any continuing role in the mediation of Christ's mysteries). Experiences of divine "absence" that were really "forms and modes of love" come together in the prophets before Christ and in the saints after him. [15]

In Eastern Orthodoxy there are openings to the notion of the Descent as a mystery of humiliation as well as of glorification. Thus Vladimir Lossky and Leonide Ouspensky in their *The Meaning of Icons*, comment on the Descent:

> Since Adam was dead, the abasement of the Saviour, Who had assumed his nature, had to reach the same depths to which Adam had descended. In other words, the descent into hell represents the very limit of Christ's degradation and, at the same time, the beginning of his glory. [16]

Kenosis and beauty belong together.

> [I]nsofar as the veil over the face of Christ's mystery is drawn aside, and insofar as the economy of grace allows, Christian contemplation can marvel, in the self-emptying of divine love, at the exceeding wisdom, truth and beauty inherent there. But it is only in this self-emptying that they can be contemplated, for it is the source whence the glory contemplated by the angels and the saints radiates into eternal life. There are "things on which the angels delight to gaze" (see I Peter 1:12), and which "the manifold wisdom of God makes known to the principalities and powers in heavenly places through the Church" (Ephesians 3:10). And if on the first Sabbath God is said to have stood back from his work and contemplated its utter rightness and goodness, so likewise the great Sabbath at the end of time, to which everything strives (Hebrews 4:1–10), will be a participation in the divine contemplation of his works (not only of God but, with God, of what God has done). [17]

The works that God has done mean above all the endlessly fruitful Sacrifice.

In sum, then—and by way of brief resolution of the theological debate mentioned above—the Descent into Hell is the last of the mysteries of humiliation and the first of the mysteries of exaltation. Christ does not only descend into Hell passively—though he does do that. When reduced to the uttermost there he becomes present actively or triumphantly too. He breaks down the "doors" by which the expectant dead were enclosed. It is from this condition that he himself rises from the grave, bringing humanity with him.

> The time for a new Sabbath arrived: the Lord, who previously had rested from the works of creation, now rested from the works of salvation. This grave, the apparent victory of death, is the victory over death. [18]

In the Byzantine-Slav icons—the mid-sixteenth-century icon of the Resurrection made for the cathedral of the Trinity at Pskov in western Russia (now in the Russian State Museum in St. Petersburg) furnishes an example— Christ is shown having left Hades, and engaged in lifting Adam and Eve to their feet, for he has rescued them from slavery to the Devil. The colors used in this icon speak of festal solemnity, they are rose-coral, emerald green, and snow white, with gleams of gold on the clothes of the witnesses of the Resurrection as well as a sheet of gold as the total background.[19] Not for nothing is the "Harrowing of Hell" scene called in Byzantine icons, *Anastasis*, "resurrection." It brings us to Easter.

NOTES

1. John Saward, *The Mysteries of March: H ans Urs von Balthasar on the Incarnation and Easter* (London: Collins, 1990), 110.

2. Saward, *The Mysteries of March*, 110.

3. "An Ancient Homily for Holy Saturday," *The Divine Office: The Liturgy of the Hours according to the Roman Rite* II, 320–21.

4. Mother Mary and Archimandrite Kallistos Ware (tr.), *The Lenten Triodion*, op, cit., 647.

5. Thomas Aquinas, *Summa theologiae*, IIIa., q. 52, a. 1.

6. For a rich comparative study of the two masters on the mysteries of Christ's life, see Etienne Vetö, *Du Christ à la Trinité*, passim.

7. Hans Urs von Balthasar, *The God-Question and Modern Man* (New York: Seabury, 1967), 133–34.

8. Hans Urs von Balthasar, *The God-Question and Modern Man*, 134.

9. Hans Urs von Balthasar, *The God-Question and Modern Man*, 134.

10. Hans Urs von Balthasar, *The God-Question and Modern Man*, 73, 75. Compare Thomas Aquinas, *Commentary on the Apostles' Creed* 5.

11. Hans Urs von Balthasar, *Explorations in Theology IV: Spirit and Institution* (San Francisco: Ignatius, 1995), 234–35.

12. Hans Urs von Balthasar, *Theo-Drama: Theological Dramatic Theory V: The Last Act*, 256–65.

13. Hans Urs von Balthasar, *Theo-Drama*, 257.

14. Hans Urs von Balthasar, *Prayer*, 164.

15. Hans Urs von Balthasar, *Prayer*, 35.

16. Vladimir Lossky and Leonid Ouspensky, *The Meaning of Icons* (Crestwood, NY: St Vladimir's Seminary Press, 1982), 187.

17. Hans Urs von Balthasar, "Revelation and the Beautiful," in *Explorations in Theology I: The Word made Flesh* (San Francisco: Ignatius, 1989), 113–14.

18. Sergius Bulgakov, *Churchly Joy Orthodox Devotions for the Church Year* (Grand Rapids, MI: Eerdmans, 2008), 107.

19. For a full description of this icon, see Irina Shalina, "The Descent into Hell (Anastasis) with Saints," in Roderick Grierson (ed.), *Gates of Mystery: The Art of Holy Russia* (Fort Worth: Intercultura, 2007), 219–25.

Chapter Eleven

Resurrection

What do the Resurrection narratives of the New Testament have to tell about the "Easter enigma"?[1] John Wenham, in a careful harmonization of the traditions contained in the four Gospels together with Paul's First Letter to Corinth, has sewn together a unitary account. His version emphasizes the distinct rationales of the appearances in Jerusalem (initially) and Galilee (subsequently).

> The initial appearances in Jerusalem were clearly important evidentially. There was great psychological value in staying around within walking distance of the empty tomb for eight days, to preclude the possibility of any later suspicion of hallucination. . . . [B]ut all this was preparatory to the great gathering in the hills of Galilee. It is this gathering to which Matthew directs almost exclusive attention. . . . Once his followers had grasped the fact that Jesus had conquered death, they would instinctively have expected him to establish his throne in *Jerusalem* without delay. To counter this reaction, the Maundy Thursday promise and the announcement on the resurrection morning direct their minds instead to *Galilee*. In Galilee the apostles were made the instrument for regathering the scattered believers, and in their presence they were recommisioned. They were re-formed as the leaders of a great company who had become witnesses of the resurrection. In the atmosphere of Galilee they were weaned afresh from the idea of a temporal Jewish Messianic kingdom, till ready to be sent back to the city which had crucified the Lord to begin their worldwide witness.[2]

A good example of his approach comes in his detective-like enquiry into the Jerusalem evidence. His report is based not only on the probable matching of names to domiciles on Easter eve (Holy Saturday evening) and not just—as would be more usual in present-day biblical scholarship—on the distinctive interests of particular evangelists. Wenham is able to establish that the evangelists are by no means confused about the identities of the "holy women" (known in the Byzantine East as the "Myrrh-bearers" or "spice-bearers"). That is important, since the women are the earliest witnesses of the Resurrection appearances. His sifting of this evidence forms part of Wenham's overall conclusion:

> These records exhibit the characteristics of accurate and independent reporting, for superficially they show great disharmony, but on close examination the details fall gradually into place. We have seen how an accurate knowledge of topography, a full acquaintance with the actors in the drama and an understanding of the differing viewpoints of the narrators, all throw light on the probable course of events. [3]

What do the Fathers and the Liturgies have to tell us? *Resurrectio* is the only mystery of the Lord that was celebrated throughout the ancient Church not only annually but weekly. Its weekly feast, of course, was Sunday. Eusebius of Caesarea explained its emergence.

> Once the Jews had proved faithless, the Word transferred the Sabbath feast to the dawn and gave us, as an image of true rest, the saving, first, Lord's day of light. This is the day on which the Saviour of the world, having accomplished all his works among us, and having overcome death, entered the gates of heaven. He thus passed beyond the creation that was made in six days, and received the blessed Sabbath and its beatific rest. [4]

In the Byzantine Liturgy, Sunday is called the "Day of the Resurrection," either stimulating or reflecting a more marked Paschal character for the day than in the other liturgical traditions. [5] But this is only one of three defining features in the Liturgies taken overall. Sunday is

> the memorial day of the resurrection, which we celebrate in faith; it is a day of expectation of the Lord's return, which we celebrate in hope; and, because Christians come together on this day and the Word of God is proclaimed, and the Eucharistic sacrifice is offered, it is a day of actual presence of the Lord among his followers, and we commune with him there in love. [6]

It is the custom of the later Church to celebrate infant Baptisms on Sundays whenever possible, thus preserving, as well as can be, the link to the adult Baptisms on Easter night.

"Resurrection" also means the great annual feast, the "sacrament" of the Lord's rising again. And here we note how the yearly celebration of the Resurrection passes into the worship of the patristic age above all through the initiation of new believers into the Paschal faith. Ildefonso Schuster noted how at Rome the entire paschal liturgy . . . was influenced by the thought of the sacrament of baptism. By virtue of its sacred laver the neophytes have been admitted to rise again from death with Christ. In order, therefore, to enter into the spirit of the liturgy of this week, it is necessary to bear always in mind the link which exists between the Pasch of Christ rising from the grave and the Pasch of the Church emerging from the font of baptism to a new and spiritual life. [7]

For Aquinas, theological elucidation of the meaning of the post-Burial events falls under the rubric of the "exaltation" of Christ, a term which covers his Resurrection, Ascension and Session (or "seating" at the Father's right).

For both Resurrection and Ascension, at any rate, Thomas will speak of the extension of these mysteries to human beings in terms of a kind of causality that is not only a matter of *efficacy*—of being an *effective* cause— but also a matter of *exemplarity*, of being an *exemplar* cause as well. When Thomas says that Christ's Resurrection was the "exemplar and cause of our resurrection,"[8] he means that the Easter event was *both* the exemplary cause *and* the efficacious cause of the rising again of the faithful. The form of Christ's glorious Easter body will communicate its character to the bodies of others, corresponding to some words of Paul, "He will transfigure these wretched bodies of ours into copies of his glorious body" (Philippians 3:21). Christ rose again *ad informationem vitae fidelium.*[9] What Thomas means is, Christ rose again in order to inform the lives of the faithful by communicating to their existence the form of his own new life as man. That can begin here and now, before the general Resurrection, since here and now it is possible to live by grace in *newness of life.* The phrase comes, once again, from St. Paul in a passage from First Corinthians that Thomas uses to explain the *information* in question. "As Christ was raised from the dead by the Father's glory, we too might live a new life" (I Corinthians 13: 12).

As St. Thomas says, there is this need of an exemplar cause, since the baptized—those justified and sanctified in regeneration—"must rise from the dead with our resurrection patterned on that of Christ."[10] The efficient causality of the Easter mystery extends to all human beings, good and evil alike, those who are to be redeemed and those who will remain reprobate. But the exemplar causality of Christ's Resurrection will apply only to those who "become fully conformed to the image of his own sonship."[11]

In fact Thomas holds that Christ's Resurrection is the origin not only of the resurrection of others but also of their justification, when they are regenerated into his new creation by faith and Baptism and begin to live the life of sanctifying grace, which is indeed the new life. For justification involves the resurrection of the soul, long before there is a prospect of the resurrection of the body. Thomas affirms that, just as the Passion and Death of Christ is the exemplar cause of the remission of our faults for we die to sin in the image of the Savior's death to the sin of the world, so his Resurrection is the exemplar cause of newness of life in us, for in justification we rise again spiritually in the image of his glorious life as shown at Easter to the first disciples. [12]

For Balthasar, the Resurrection is both historical and "meta-historical," both an empirical disclosure, made so that we may grasp the meaning of salvation-history as a whole, and an event that "withdraws itself from our gaze," because it takes the form of a "return to the Father, to eternity." [13]

> The Father is the Creator who, acting at Easter in The Son, brings his work to completion; the Father, in exalting his Son, also brings the Son's mission to its completion, and makes the Son visible to the world, spreading abroad the Spirit which is common to them both. [14]

And what Balthasar portrays on the broad canvas of his great exegetical and doctrinal study of the events of the first Easter, *Mysterium Paschale*, he reiterates in the devotional cameo of his Rosary meditation in *The Threefold Garland*. The Resurrection is an act of the entire Holy Trinity.

> The Resurrection is a trinitarian event. With his death on the cross, the Son of God fulfilled his mandate; with his human spirit he gave back to the Father also the Spirit of his mission. As a man he cannot himself rise from the dead; it is the Father who, as "the God of the living" (Romans 4:17) awakens the Son from among the dead, so that he, as one freshly united with the Father, can send forth God's Spirit into the Church. [15]

Bulgakov echoes this interrelation of Easter and Pentecost: "The Resurrection is Christ's Pentecost, the descent of the life-giving Holy Spirit on the Divine deceased." [16] And because this divine "dead One" was the New Adam, who freely took on himself the death-dealing abandonment of the human race by the Spirit of God, in his death that Spirit returns to man who thus attains once more the fullness of life.

What of Resurrection iconography? It is admitted that the eighteenth-century Dionysius of Fourna's *The Painter's Manual* was not reporting the tradition correctly when it called the *Anastasis* icon "The Descent of the Lord to Adam" (though the mistake continues to be made). The binding of Satan, key to the theme of the Harrowing of Hell (as distinct from the Resurrection of Christ), does not appear until the late period in Byzantine iconography, usually under Western influence. The standard or classical *Anastasis* image takes the Resurrection of Christ himself as having happened already. In other words, this is not exactly Holy Saturday. It is Easter Day, or at any rate Easter night. It is perfectly true, however, that the restoration of Adam is central to the Byzantine Easter icon. The theologically gifted art historian Anna Kartsonis wrote,

The recognition of Adam by homilists as "the first created and the first dead among men" makes his raising from the dead an act of recreation on the part of the Logos. This in turn is interpreted as signifying the opening of the era of Redemption for mankind, achieved through the Incarnation, the Passion and the Death of Christ. Thus in the image of the *Anastasis*, Adam stands for Everyman. His Resurrection declares the availability of Resurrection to all mankind, a vital doctrine of the Church.[17]

St. Gregory the Theologian had declared of Easter, "With us it is the feast of feasts and the celebration of celebrations; it excels all other festivals, as the sun excels the stars; and this is true not only of human and earthly feasts, but also of those belonging to Christ and celebrated for Christ."[18]

That icon is complemented by another, which portrays the visit to the tomb of the Lord of the Myrrh-bearing (or Spice-bearing) Women. They had expected to find the tomb as they had left it. But it was no ordinary tomb. The dead body that had lain there was the body of the divine Word in whom is life. More wonderful even than that he should demonstrate just a little of his power by raising it to life was that he should suffer it to lie so docile to created powers. The ultimate cause, after all, is present in all other causes: it is by his power that any other cause is a cause at all. As to the Byzantine-Slav icon, Ouspensky describes it as so simple it might almost be called "ordinary," except that an angel—or angels—is present.[19] The tomb is shown with the discarded garments described in the Gospels and the women to one side. The number not only of angels but also of spice bearers varies, according to which Gospel book is being followed.

Both Nyssa and Palamas thought there was more than one visit, hence none of the number counts is necessarily wrong. In the seventeenth century, Russian artists under Western influence include at the top of the icon a smaller scene where the risen Christ stands among little hills and greets Mary Magdalene who, in St. John's Gospel, takes him for the gardener. Ouspensky thought the decision to show with the Magdalene a Christ dressed in ordinary garments derived from a desire not to seek to depict the ineffable moment of the Resurrection itself. The "idea" is the same as in later Western art, which does not scruple to show him in the moment of rising, but the "form" is significantly different.[20] The Resurrection is not resuscitation (though it includes resuscitation). It is a meta-event, changing the conditions of existence for Christ and the cosmos and thus, properly speaking, lies beyond depiction.

NOTES

1. John Wenham, *Easter Enigma* (Exeter: Paternoster Press, 1984).
2. Ibid., 122, 123.
3. Ibid., 124.
4. Eusebius, *Commentary on Psalm 91*.

5. Irénée-Henri Dalmais, O. P., "Le dimanche dans la Liturgie byzantine," *La Maison-Dieu* 46 (1956), 60–66.

6. Irénée-Henri Dalmais, Pierre Jounel, and Aimé Georges Martimort, *The Church at Prayer, An Introduction to the Liturgy, IV: The Liturgy and Time*, 18.

7. Ildefonso Schuster, *The Sacramentary (Liber Sacramentorum): Historical and Liturgical Notes on the Roman Missal* (London: Burns, Oates and Washbourne, 1924), II., 308–9.

8. Thomas Aquinas, *Summa theologiae*, IIIa., q. 54, a. 2.

9. Ibid., IIIa., q. 53, a. 1.

10. Ibid., IIIa., q. 56, a. 1, ad iii.

11. Ibid.

12. Ibid., IIIa., q. 56, a. 2, ad iv.

13. Hans Urs von Balthasar, *Mysterium Paschale*, 189.

14. Ibid.

15. Hans Urs von Balthasar, *The Threefold Garland*, 109–10.

16. Sergius Bulgakov, *Churchly Joy: Orthodox Devotions for the Church Year* (Grand Rapids, MI: Eerdmans, 2008), 120.

17. Anna Kartsonis, *Anastasis, the Making of an Image* (Princeton: Princeton University Press, 1986), 5, with an internal citation from the Pseudo-Epiphanius, *De sancto et magno Sabbato*.

18. Gregory Nazianzen, *Easter Sermon* 45, in Vladimir Lossky and Leonid Ouspensky, *The Meaning of Icons* (Crestwood, NY: St Vladimir's Seminary Press, 1982), 185.

19. Ibid., 191.

20. Ibid., 188, fn 4.

Chapter Twelve

Ascension

Michael Ramsey, writing of the biblical data for the Ascension mystery, found no better general statement than one from the least known of the great trio of late Victorian Anglican exegetes, Lightfoot, Westcott, and Hort:

> "As yet it was hardly possible for them to feel the difference between His being with them where they were, and their being with Him where He was. . . . *that* was the transition now coming, the transition from a presence taking its character from their circumstances to a presence taking its character from His." [Ramsey commented on Hort's words:] In the new era which will follow His departure He will receive the disciples that "where I am they may be also" (John 14:3), and while the disciples will find mansions . . . in the Father's house, the Father and the Son will come and make their dwelling . . . in the disciples (14:23).[1]

In the Ascension event, the Lord's account of glorification in his High Priestly Prayer at the Supper comes into its own. At first sight, that Prayer is riddling. The Son affirms he has enjoyed glory from the Father from before the world was made, and yet he asks that glory may be given him in his Passion and the Exaltation that follows. Ramsey's solution is elegant. "It is by the humiliation of the Son's winning of glory in the toils of history that the eternal glory of the divine self-giving is most signally disclosed.[2] "

After the forty days the crucified and risen Lord withdraws, then, from what the physicists would call our space-time continuum. He goes to constitute a new set of coordinates for reality: the new creation, the cosmos or world order of the Age to Come, which by definition is not yet. In the Johannine Apocalypse, *the* "revelation"—the "apocalypse" or "unveiling" from which the book gets its name—comes when a curtain is thrown back before the seer's eyes to disclose an open doorway into heaven (Apocalypse

4:1), a door that opens onto the new space-time of the ascended Lord. And there at the center of heavenly space, St. John, the beloved disciple, sees Christ once more. But he seems him under the species of a lamb, a lamb bearing the marks of its executioners' blows. The lamb in question is not, however, flat out on an abattoir floor. Rather, it is a lamb that is standing—standing, we are expected to understand, proudly erect (Apocalypse 5:6). The Lamb that was slain and stands erect is Scripture's supreme image of the ascended Christ. In his Ascension glory, Jesus is the Lord of love, and not just the Victim of love. He remains the Crucified, but he is the Crucified as One who has been given "all authority in heaven and on earth" (Matthew 28:18). He is reigning, and wherever love like his, sacrificial love that mirrors the kenotic communion of the Holy Trinity, prevails on earth, there his Kingdom, which is the Father's Kingdom, has already come.

How did the ancient Fathers and Liturgies see the Ascension mystery and its celebration? The documentary evidence for the celebration of the feast is no earlier than a canon of the (Spanish) Council of Elvira from around the year 300, and a discussion by Eusebius some years later that brackets together the Ascension and Pentecost.[3] Yet by the time of Augustine of Hippo Ascension Day was "already so universally observed . . . that St. Augustine was able to attribute its institution to the Apostles themselves."[4] Its principal distinguishing mark was a solemn procession around mid-day in commemoration of how the apostles had accompanied the Savior to the Mount of Olives—originally a Jerusalem specialty for a combined festivity of Ascension and Pentecost, witnessed by the pilgrim Egeria on her travels. The feast ushered in a period of intensified rejoicing and prayer, the original "novena." St. John Cassian insists that "[t]he ten days between the Ascension and Pentecost must be celebrated with the same solemnity and joy as the forty days that preceded them."[5]

In North Africa, Augustine's very full preaching on this topic, found in *Sermons* 261 to 265, opens with the words "The resurrection of the Lord is our hope; the Lord's ascension our glorification."[6] We have been joined in the Church to the Lord's embodied humanity; this is the key. "Although he came down without a body [he] ascended with a body, and we too are going to ascend, not by our own prowess, but by our and his oneness. "Two," indeed, "in one flesh; it is a great sacrament in Christ and in the Church."[7]

At Rome, St. Leo presented the Ascension mystery in two sermons later joined together as a single "tractate."[8] The Ascension is the elevation of our nature to the Father, viewed with amazement by the cosmic powers.

> And truly great and unspeakable was their cause for joy, when in the sight of the holy multitude, above the dignity of all heavenly creatures, the nature of humankind went up, to pass above the angels' ranks and to rise beyond the archangels' heights, and to have its uplifting limited by no elevation until,

received to sit with the eternal Father, it should be associated on the throne with his glory, to whose nature it was united in the Son.[9]

All human nature is "glorified in the glorification of Christ."[10] But, as Armitage stresses in his study of Leo's soteriology, this claim must not be misunderstood. Christians have entered into consubstantiality with Christ through the new birth of Baptism and their flesh is thus suitable for coglorification with the ascended Lord's. Nevertheless, they have to maintain the integrity of the new birth, to "walk in the way of *conversatio sancta* and *doctrina divina*"—living as true disciples morally, by *occisio vitiorum*, the "slaying of the vices," and doctrinally, by *abdicatio omnis erroris*, "abdication of all error."[11] In this way they will present no obstacle to sharing Jesus's glory.

What, for the great theologians of later times, can the Ascension add to the Resurrection mystery that, after all, is already the exaltation of the Crucified? In Thomas's account, Christ's body does not become more exalted at the Ascension but precisely in its exalted condition it now becomes more at home, being as it is, thanks to the Ascension mystery, in the heavenly places. When he tells the disciples in the Last Supper discourse that it is for their good that he is going (compare John 16:7), so as to prepare a place for them (John 14:2), Thomas understands this to mean that by his Ascension the Lord prepares the way for his disciples to join him in heaven, "initiating as our Head what we his members share in union with him." His Ascension is "directly the cause" writes Thomas, of the ascension of human being,[12] a perfect example of his mystery becoming the mystery of Christians, or, in Abbot Marmion's favored phrase "our mystery."

Marmion himself wrote,

> Even though Christ no longer merits now, His Ascension nevertheless has the power of producing efficaciously the graces it signifies or symbolizes. It strengthens our faith in the divinity of Jesus; it increases our hope through the sight of the glory of our head. By animating us to observe His commandments—this observance being the basis of our merits, which themselves are the source of our future beatitude—it makes our love more ardent. It engenders in us admiration for so marvelous a triumph, and gratitude for the sharing in it that Christ gives us. Raising our souls toward heavenly things, it brings alive in them detachment from things that are passing. "If you have risen with Christ, seek the things that are above, where Christ is seated at the right hand of God . . . not the things that are on earth" [Colossians 3:1–2]. It gives us patience with the adversities of here below. For, as St. Paul says, if we have shared the sufferings of Christ, we shall be associated also with His glory: "sharing His sufferings so as to share His glory" [Romans 8:17].[13]

Balthasar's understanding of the Ascension also links it to the Incarnation—not simply as divine pedagogy but in its full saving reality.

> Something heavenly was sown into the earth, and the one now returning to the
> Father, being the heavenly Head of the still earthly Church, henceforth estab-
> lishes an indissoluble bond between earth and heaven.[14]

But this also entails a demand.

> For the time being the Head of the church has been raised up to God so that the
> Church should exert herself for existing within the huge expanses of her prop-
> er habitation in God. For, seen from below, a distance is created which awak-
> ens and intensifies our yearning; but this distance is one that is lived in God—
> spent in believing, hoping and loving—so that it is an intensification of the
> divine life in those that remain behind.[15]

For Bulgakov the Ascension mystery, since it signifies the ultimate glorification of human nature, belongs with those of both Christmas and Easter,
both Nativity and Resurrection.

> The Ascension is the power of Christ's Birth, for it signifies the indissolubility
> of the divine and human essence. The Ascension is the power of the Resurrec-
> tion, which would not have been completed if the Resurrected One did not
> acquire the power to ascend to heaven with His most pure flesh.[16]

The Byzantine icons of the Ascension place at least as much stress on the
significance, and consequences, the Ascension has for the world as on its
reality as the event whereby Christ reaches his destiny at the Father's right.
Though the olive trees frequently depicted on the icons suggest the historical
facticity of the event at its this-worldly pole, the "mandorla," consisting of
several concentric circles, symbolic of the highest heavens, in which Christ is
enveloped indicates that the ascending Savior enters meta-history—and
meta-geography as well! Among the apostles stands, centrally placed, and
sometimes on a slight eminence to show her higher dignity, the Mother of
God whom the evangelist Luke does not, however, mention in this context,
either in his Gospel book or in the Acts of the Apostles. Her presence is,
nonetheless, clearly affirmed by the liturgical tradition. "Rejoice thou Mother
of Christ our God, seeing with the apostles him, whom thou didst engender
ascending to heaven and glorifying him."[17] The immobility of Mary
contrasts with the animated, gesticulating apostles. Ouspensky wrote, "This
group, with the Mother of God at its center, represents our Savior's inheritance, gained by His blood—the Church He was physically leaving behind
on earth, which, through the promised descent of the Holy Spirit at the
coming Pentecost, would receive all the fullness of its being."[18] Her arms
uplifted in intercession, or on her breast, palms outward, as a witness, she
personifies the Church and for that reason stands immediately below the
ascending Lord. With his right hand he blesses, with his left he holds a scroll
or book. Thus, while dwelling in heaven, he remains the source of blessing,

yes, but also of knowledge, as communicated to the Church by the Holy Spirit. The icon of the Ascension is a prophetic icon, for the angels tell the apostles the Lord will return—in judgment—in the same way as they have seen him leave, which is why the icons of the Parousia—the *Secundus Adventus*, "second Coming"—echo those of the Ascension. The Christ Pantokrator maintains, moreover, the form of the double-handed blessing and teaching, so this is for the in-between times and not just the End.

NOTES

1. Arthur Michael Ramsey, *The Glory of God and the Transfiguration of Christ* (London: Darton, Longman and Todd, 1967 [1949]), 73, citing F. J. A. Hort, *The Way, the Truth, the Life* (Cambridge and New York: MacMillan, 1893), 14.

2. Arthur Michael Ramsey, *The Glory of God and the Transfiguration of Christ*, 86.

3. Eusebius, *On the Paschal Solemnity*, 3. See Irénée-Henri Dalmais, Pierre Jounel, and Aimé Georges Martimort, *The Church at Prayer, An Introduction to the Liturgy, IV: The Liturgy and Time* (London: Chapman, 1986), 59.

4. Ildefonso Schuster, *The Sacramentary (Liber Sacramentorum): Historical and Liturgical Notes on the Roman Missal* (London: Burns, Oates and Washbourne, 1924), II., 374. See Augustine, *Sermon* 362.

5. John Cassian, *Conferences* 21, 19–20.

6. Augustine, *Sermon* 261. See for the series, John E. Rotelle, O. S. A. (ed.), *The Works of Saint Augustine: Sermons III/7 On the Liturgical Seasons* (New Rochelle, NY: New City Press, 1993), 208–66.

7. Augustine, *Sermon* 263A, with an internal citation of Ephesians 5:31–32.

8. Leo, *Sermon* 73.

9. Leo, *Sermon* 73.

10. J. Mark Armitage, *A Twofold Solidarity: Leo the Great's Theology of Redemption* (Strathfield, NSW: St Paul's Publications, 2005), 123.

11. Armitage, *A Twofold Solidarity*, 124, glossed in the light of pp. 112–13.

12. Thomas Aquinas, *Summa theologiae*, IIIa., q. 57, a. 6, ad ii.

13. Columba Marmion, *Christ in His Mysteries* (Bethesda, MD: Zacchaeus Press, 2008), 359.

14. Hans Urs von Balthasar, *The Threefold Garland* (San Francisco, CA: Ignatius, 1982), 115–16.

15. Hans Urs von Balthasar, *The Threefold Garland*, 117.

16. Sergius Bulgakov, *Churchly Joy: Orthodox Devotions for the Church Year* (Grand Rapids, MI: Eerdmans, 2008), 123.

17. Cited from the Byzantine Liturgy in Vladimir Lossky and Leonid Ouspensky, *The Meaning of Icons* (Crestwood, NY: St Vladimir's Seminary Press, 1982), 196.

18. Lossky and Ouspensky, *The Meaning of Icons*, 196.

Chapter Thirteen

Pentecost

The Parousia is proleptically present by virtue of Pentecost, but it is so only on the basis of the Paschal Mystery. In the *Evolution of the Christian Year*, Allan McArthur explained the relation of Pentecost to the events of the Passion and Resurrection.

> Just as the Old Covenant established in the Exodus and remembered at Passover was fulfilled on Sinai, so the New Covenant established in the events remembered by the Christian Passover was fulfilled on Pentecost. The Christian Pentecost became the birthday of the Church as the New Israel of God. [1]

This is no more than a summary of the data of Scripture. The Pentecostal descent of the Holy Spirit, sent by the Son from the Father, renders fully actual in human beings the Savior's work. That makes Pentecost a clear example of a mystery of Christ that is to become a mystery of our own. In the words of a mid-twentieth-century bishop of Rome, "[W]hile Christ alone received the Spirit without measure, it is only according to the measure of the giving of Christ and from the fullness of Christ himself that he is bestowed upon the members of the mystical Body. And since Christ has been glorified on the Cross his Spirit is communicated to the Church in abundant outpouring, in order that she and each of her members may grow daily in likeness to our Saviour. It is the Spirit of Christ who has made us adopted sons of God, so that one day 'we all, beholding the glory of the Lord with open face, may be transformed into the same image from glory to glory.'"[2] Thus this mystery fulfills the divine plan for humanity—the "Adam" created to be the temple of the Holy Spirit, not, though, without the natural cosmos but with it, since he was to be its soul and its priest.

Alexander Schmemann, also writing as one wearing the cap of a biblical theologian, looks not only back but forward, linking Pentecost to the Parousia, for the "eighth day" of which he writes can only be, in the last analysis, the eschatologically expected "Day of the Lord."

> Through his coming on the "last and great day of Pentecost" the Holy Spirit transforms this *last* day into the first day of the new creation and manifests the Church as the gift and presence of this first and "eighth" day.[3]

For when the Fathers speak of the mystery of the "eighth day," they have in mind an "anticipation of eternal life."[4]

These are the themes, at once Paschal and "Parousial," that at Pentecost preoccupy the Fathers and the ancient Liturgies. In Rome, as the procession at the baptisteries on Whitsun Eve wended its way to the font, the Church refreshed her memory of the sacramental initiations that had taken place at the Easter Vigil. But her singers were chanting in that procession the opening verses of Psalm 42 with its yearning for seeing the divine Face at the end of time. "As a hart longs for flowing streams, so longs my soul for thee, O God. My soul thirsts for God, the living God. When shall I come and behold the face of God?" (Psalm 42:1–3). And in the collect that followed their arrival, the celebrant prayed, "Grant, we beseech thee, O almighty God: that we who celebrate the solemnity of the gift of the Holy Spirit, being inflamed with heavenly desires, may thirst after the fountain of life."[5]

At Constantinople, however, Pentecost Sunday became in due course the Byzantine rite's equivalent of the Trinity Sunday of the West. The celebration of the Descent of the Holy Spirit for its own sake was postponed there until the day following. This development had a plain rationale. Pentecost completes the formation of the Church founded in the Paschal Mystery. But, precisely in doing so, it also fulfills the revelation of God the Holy Trinity.

The classic Western patristic theology of Pentecost can be found in the sermons of Augustine and Leo. Under the influence of his struggle with Donatism, Augustine, in his sermons on Pentecost, emphasizes the unity the Spirit brings.[6] They are the dissidents he has in his mind as a contrast to the faithful at Hippo. "You, though, my brothers and sisters, members of the body of Christ, seedlings of unity, sons and daughter of peace, keep this day joyfully celebrate it without anxiety. Among you, after all, is being fulfilled what was being prefigured in those days, when the Holy Spirit came.[7] " As to Leo, he stresses the "rain of charismatic gifts" that has poured out on the Church, with power to enlighten, to create understanding, and to burn away sin.[8]

In the East, St. Gregory Nazianzen cries out in his first Easter Oration, "May he that rose today from the dead also recreate me by the Spirit."[9] Winslow comments, "That is, the new creation effected by the work of Christ, in his assumption of our common nature, life and death, is communicated individually—'to me'—by the Spirit. Gregory uses many words to define the nature of the re-creative activity of the Spirit, all of them drawn from the New Testament: the Spirit is perfecter, fulfiller, and sanctifier. The Spirit's deity rests, ultimately, for Gregory, on these functions, a deity that is not 'by adoption' but 'by nature,' a deity not all his own but of the essence of the godhead. For what the Spirit does is precisely what God does."[10] Cyril of Alexandria does justice to the holism of the Spirit's gift in his *Commentary on the Gospel of John*: "[W]hile Christ was still present in bodily form among those who believed in him, he was revealed to them as one who conferred every good gift; but since the time and the need were now calling him to be carried up to his Father in heaven, it was necessary for him to be present through the Spirit with those who worshipped him, and to dwell in our hearts through faith. Having him within us in this way, we would be able to cry out with confidence: 'Abba, Father!,' and to make peaceful progress towards every virtue; we would prove powerful and invincible against the wiles of the devil and the attacks of men, for we would possess the Spirit whose power has no limit."[11]

For St. Thomas, the same Holy Spirit who conforms human beings to Christ, making them truly "in the image" of God, after the model of Jesus— the "Image" par excellence, is given only to those who are already "in Christ" by their faith in the Son's Death and Exaltation. "As the life-giving natural breath does not reach the member that is not connected to its head, in the same way the Holy Spirit does not reach the member who is not con- nected with his head, Christ."[12] The Dominican theologian Jean-Pierre Tor- rell explains Thomas's logic here. "Because of the primary Trinitarian origin and the circumincession of the divine Persons, there is a reciprocal condition of their action and, according to the point of view the priority will differ in each case."[13] In the mystery of the Baptism, the Son was sent by the Spirit. Now, in the mystery of Pentecost, the Spirit is sent by the Son.

For Aquinas, the economy of the Spirit is as appropriate for the comple- tion of our salvation, just as was the economy of the Son for the creation and its redemptive repair. And "appropriate" here means—in the last analysis— in keeping with the Trinitarian processions. For the missions of the Persons in time truly to embody the processions of the Persons in eternity it was "necessary that the Father's Love, directed toward the Son as its object, would be the reason by which God bestows each of love's effects on the creature. That is why the Holy Spirit, who is the Love by which the Father loves the Son, is also the Love by which He loves the creature and imparts to it His perfection."[14] The plenitude of the Son's generous self-gift to the Father for the world is now matched by the fullness of the Spirit's bestowal from Father and Son. In more Thomistic language, "since it is in the Holy Spirit and through Him that the Father and the Son love each other and love creatures, it is also in Him and through Him that their movement of return toward the Father is completed."[15] Since the Spirit is one and the same in the

Head and the members he can deploy for this purpose the grace of the Head until the end of time.

Speaking for the great masters of later theology, Balthasar explains how Pentecost is made possible only by the Paschal Mystery. The English theologian John Saward, expounding the thought of the Swiss dogmatician, wrote, "Only when the Son, by the motion of the Spirit, has breathed out his life and love for the Father and all mankind, only when the Father has accepted his Sacrifice and poured out the Spirit on his humanity in the Resurrection, only then can the risen Lord breathe the Spirit on the apostles (John 20:22); only then can the Dove descend from the Father and the Son upon the whole Church at Pentecost."[16] Balthasar himself wrote in a Pentecost sermon, "On the Cross the Son of God's heart was pierced and there flowed out blood and water (the source of the sacraments); but in reality the spear pierced right through to his soul, his 'I,' 'right to the knot of the Trinity' (as [Paul] Claudel puts it); now, therefore, God's Spirit pours forth into the world as from a leaking jar."[17] Balthasar apologizes for the coarseness of the image but says it is justified by the need to realize the "tangibility" of what is happening. Even the "rushing mighty wind" experienced by those in the Upper Room and the "tongues of fire" that descended on them, *realia*—not literary tropes—as they were, can only be considered in comparison with the Descent itself "metaphors for an elemental event, elemental as were only the events of creation (where we were not present) and of redemption, from crib to Cross (which we did not understand)."[18] The something that happened was that "man is enabled to share in the Spirit's proceeding from Father and Son," a sharing we call the "fulness of sanctifying grace."[19] Pentecost depends here on the Ascension, as Balthasar explains in his book on prayer—a book that is also a treatise on the Holy Trinity. "Caught up . . . to the 'right hand of the Father,' the Son's transfigured humanity becomes involved in the eternal spiration of the Holy Spirit, and the immediate consequence of this is that the Spirit is poured out into Christ's mystical body on earth."[20]

For his part, Bulgakov lets the Pentecost event throw light on the wider presence of the Spirit in the cosmic creation, and the creation of man in particular, as well as in the history of Israel, before reaching the highpoint of that history in the Annunciation to Blessed Mary.[21] Yet not until the Baptism of Christ and, above all, not until his Ascension with its completing of the Paschal Mystery, is the Spirit able to descend in totally transformative fashion.

> Only from heaven, having fully deified and glorified the human essence, does the Son of Man send from the Heavenly Father the Holy Spirit upon all humanity, just as and because upon His human essence as well was sent the Holy Spirit, who reposes upon him.[22]

In iconography, following the cues the Byzantine Liturgy gives, we need to distinguish between the Pentecost icon of the Trinity, on the one hand, and, on the other, the icon of the Descent of the Holy Spirit—as celebrated in and for itself. In the festal icon for the day following Pentecost, devoted as this is to the descent of the Spirit on the Church, the Pentecost event appears as the "baptism of the Church by fire."[23] "The icon of the Descent of the Holy Spirit reveals the providential action of the Holy Trinity in relation to the Church and the world."[24] In this icon, the serene, harmonious placing of the apostles, arranged in a semi-circle, bears witness to how the Church, like the Trinity, is to be a unity in plurality. An empty central seat is reserved for Christ, the invisible Head of the Church, for the Church the apostles represent is the mystical Body of the Savior, the Trinitarian Son. From a segment of the circle surmounting the icon come tongues of fire that are a "sign of baptism with the Holy Spirit and with fire, according to the prophecy of John the Forerunner (Matthew 3:11), and a sign too of [the apostles'] sanctification."[25] Some of the apostles hold books, others have scrolls. In either case they show they are the legitimate teachers of the Church. In ancient illuminations, the whole multitude of the Church might appear gathered beneath the apostles. In later icons they are replaced by a crowned figure who (on one interpretation) stands for the royal priesthood of all the baptized.

But Pentecost is not only about the descent of the Spirit on the Church. It is also the celebration of that consummate revelation of the Holy Trinity that the Paschal Mystery makes possible. Indeed, for Hans Urs von Balthasar, the feast of the Trinity "joins the others, not as the recalling of some particular, recondite mystery that needs to be brought to mind once a year but as the sum of them all—Christmas, Good Friday, Easter, Ascension, Pentecost— finally allowing us to see together, in a unity, what up to now we saw as a colourful spectrum of broken light."[26] As he explains,

> The Father can give us the Son to be "with" us at a human level—the Son's eternal proceeding from the Father is continued in the dimension of time—but when the Son takes us with him into his communion ("being with") the Father, he does so in a way that opens us to the cascading stream of the life of the absolute "With," namely, the Holy Spirit.[27]

So Balthasar might well concur with the Byzantine East: the chief task of Pentecost Sunday is to exhibit—and to praise—the dogma of the Trinity. Its festal icon is the "angelic" Trinity at the oaks of Mamre, from the Abraham cycle in the book of Genesis. The Fathers of the Church interpret Abraham's three visitors, who in the narrative are sometimes addressed as one, as an indication of the reality of the Trinity, whether as Father, Son, and Spirit or as the Word accompanied by two angels—still numbering a threesome, of course. St. Andrei Rublev's transformation of the inherited iconographic

tradition is especially eloquent, as we shall see. The East has no feast of the
Trinity such as was introduced in the Latin Church in 1334, but in Russia,

> Pentecost acquired with time the character of a feast of the Holy Trinity. It has
> often been assumed, probably with good reason, that this happened under the
> influence of the Trinitarian mysticism of St. Sergii of Radonezh, the fullest
> pictorial expression of which is found in Rublev's *Troitsa*. Through this link
> between Pentecost and the *mysterium Trinitatis*, Rublev's Trinity icon and
> other similar icons equally attain the rank of a festal icon..[28]

In the light of this icon, one can see the feast of the Holy Trinity as a
"deepening of the festal mystery of Pentecost."[29]

The peculiarity of Rublev's icon is that he has not followed precedent by
painting either "one individual form with two companions" (a primarily
Christological icon) or an icon with "three equal interchangeable forms" (a
"standard Trinitarian icon"), but an icon that shows "three non-interchange-
able persons."[30] This means that the "question as to the identity of the three
angelic forms—however fruitless it may be in the case of the predecessors of
Rublev and also of most of his followers" is, according to this interpreter,
Hieromonk Gabriel Bunge, here "unavoidable."[31] Rublev's icon with its cir-
cular movement of heads and gestures indicates the *perichoresis* of the divine persons. But which is which?

On one interpretation, the color scheme chosen by Rublev favors an explanation that sees the Father on the left (indefinite hues, purplish, pinkish,
brownish, blueish-green suggestive of incomprehensibility), the Son in the
middle (the purple *chiton* and blue cloak are classic for Christ), the Spirit at
the right (green, surely, for the Lifegiver), while the nearly identical faces
and figures signify the unity of the divine substance. And in terms of placing
and gesture we notice that the angel on the left "alone sits upright, while the
other two incline towards him. He thus symbolizes the Father, from whom
the Son and the Spirit go forth in their own ineffable way, but to whom they
also lead the whole creation."[32] The purple-and-gold embroidered robe of the
angel in the middle position manifests kingship as the anointed one, while his
cloak can be considered a prophet's mantle, an overgarment of deep blue
unlike the largely hidden pale blue undergarment of the Father—for the Son
has *revealed* the Father's glory. The central angel also points to the chalice
with the sacrificed calf, while behind him rises the oak of Mamre here, in this
de-historicized version of the genesis story, suggesting in symbol the Tree of
the Cross. The angel on the right, leaving as he does one arm free, shows
himself to be with the central angel one of the two "hands" of the Father
spoken of by St. Irenaeus. The Spirit's overgarment is pale green, in Russia
the liturgical color of Pentecost when churches are decorated with greenery.
The rock behind him may represent the earth that the Holy Spirit is to renew.
Bunge makes much of what he admits is an "apparently trifling detail," the

Son's pointing to the Spirit with one finger—this has been disfigured by retouching, which added another finger making his gesture one of blessing, not, as it should be, of indication.

> The Son's gesture of pointing to the Spirit makes clear that the attention of the painter is directed at the Spirit, in contrast to the pattern of composition that shows the Son, traditionally, as the focal point. The Father's posture and gesture confirm this, for the Father, apparently, returns neither the gaze nor the gesture of the Son, but looks at the Spirit, to whom his right hand, raised in blessing, is directed. The Spirit, finally, bows his head humbly before the Father, and his right hand, lowered towards the table, seems to want to underline this movement. [33]

The icon in its entirety is a depiction of the Johannine Farewell Discourse, looking to the other Paraclete who will witness to the Son until he comes again. Bunge comments on John 20:19–23, a text sometimes known as the "Johannine Pentecost":

> In an infinitely tender way, Andrei Rublev understood how to make this Johannine Pentecost manifest. The movement between the three divine persons, the intra-Trinitarian conversation, proceeds from the Son: With entreaty he looks at the Father, while his right hand points to the chalice of his Passion and beyond that to the Spirit. This look and this gesture intimate the request for the sending of the Paraclete, which only becomes possible through the self-sacrifice of the Son. The Father, who always hears the Son (Jn 11:42) fulfils this request: His gaze is directed to the Spirit, who in enthroned with him behind the altar table, and his right hand bestows on him the blessing for the completion of the saving work of the Son. The Holy Spirit, however, bows his head in humble assent, which is shown by his lowered right hand. Behind the Paraclete, the rock—probably represented as cracked by Rublev—suggests in a symbol that the life-giving streams of the Holy Spirit pour forth from the opened side of the mystical rock, that is, Christ. [34]

And "[t]hanks to this personal gift and indwelling of the Spirit, there develops what we call the spiritual life" or "Christian existence."[35]

Begun in initiation into the Baptism of Christ, the first gift of the Spirit of Pentecost to any new believer in the mysteries of the Incarnation wrought at the Annunciation and Nativity, it can only make progress by an imitation of Christ based on participation in the remaining mysteries. This will mean, then, *askesis*—a voluntary suffering combined with contemplation—and philanthropy—a generous charity toward others, for these are participation in the mystery of the Passion, Death, and Descent. It will conclude, as do the mysteries themselves, in a share in the Resurrection and Ascension in *theosis*, divinization—seeing God in a renewed creation—in the Age to Come.

NOTES

1. Allan McArthur, *The Evolution of the Christian Year* (London: SCM Press, 1953), 143.

2. Pius XII, *Mystici Corporis Christi*, 54, with an internal citation of Second Corinthians 3:18.

3. Alexander Schmemann, *The Eucharist, Sacrament of the Kingdom* (Crestwood, NY: St. Vladimir''s Seminary Press, 1987), 36.

4. Irénée-Henri Dalmais, Pierre Jounel, and Aimé Georges Martimort, *The Church at Prayer, An Introduction to the Liturgy, IV: The Liturgy and Time*, (London: Chapman, 1986), 58.

5. Cited in Ildefonso Schuster, *The Sacramentary (Liber Sacramentorum): Historical and Liturgical Notes on the Roman Missal* (London: Burns, Oates and Washbourne, 1924), II., 384–85.

6. Augustine, *Sermons* 266–72b.

7. Augustine, *Sermon* 271.

8. Leo, *Sermon* 75.

9. Gregory Nazianzen, *Oration* 1. 2.

10. Donald F. Winslow, *The Dynamics of Salvation: A Study in Gregory of Nazianzus* (Cambridge, MA: Philadelphia Patristic Foundation, 1979), 130.

11. Cyril, *Commentary on the Gospel of John*, book 10, with an internal citation of Romans 8:15. The translation is from *The Divine Office. The Liturgy of the Hours according to the Roman Rite* II (London and Glasgow: Collins, 1974), 684.

12. Thomas Aquinas, *Commentary on Romans*, VIII, 2, lectio 1.

13. Jean-Pierre Torrell, O. P., *Saint Thomas Aquinas: Volume 2, Spiritual Master*, (Washington, DC: Catholic University of America Press, 2003), 148.

14. Thomas Aquinas, *Writing on the Sentences*, I., dist. 14, q. 1., a. 1.

15. Torrell, *Saint Thomas Aquinas: Volume 2, Spiritual Master*, 178.

16. John Saward, *The Mysteries of March Hans Urs von Balthasar on the Incarnation and Easter* (London: Collins, 1990), 25–26.

17. Hans Urs von Balthasar, *You Crown the Year with Your Goodness* (San Francisco: Ignatius, 1982), 137.

18. Hans Urs von Balthasar, *You Crown the Year*, 137–38.

19. Hans Urs von Balthasar, *You Crown the Year*, 138.

20. Hans Urs von Balthasar, *Prayer* (San Francisco, CA: Ignatius, 1986), 69–70.

21. Sergius Bulgakov, *Churchly Joy Orthodox Devotions for the Church Year* (Grand Rapids, MI: Eerdmans, 2008), 128.

22. Bulgakov, *Churchly Joy*, 128–29.

23. Vladimir Lossky and Leonid Ouspensky, *The Meaning of Icons* (Crestwood, NY: St Vladimir's Seminary Press, 1982), 207.

24. Lossky and Ouspensky, *The Meaning of Icons*, 207.

25. Lossky and Ouspensky, *The Meaning of Icons*, 207.

26. Hans Urs von Balthasar, *You Crown the Year*, 141.

27. Hans Urs von Balthasar, *You Crown the Year*, 144.

28. Gabriel Bunge, *Rublev's Trinity* (Crestwood, NY: St. Vladimir's Seminary Press, 2007), 79.

29. Bunge, *Rublev's Trinity*, 79.

30. Bunge, *Rublev's Trinity*, 87.

31. Bunge, *Rublev's Trinity*, 89.

32. Bunge, *Rublev's Trinity*, 96.

33. Bunge, *Rublev's Trinity*, 102.

34. Bunge, *Rublev's Trinity*, 105.

35. Bunge, *Rublev's Trinity*, 106.

Chapter Fourteen

Parousia

It is time to turn to the future Parousia: the Second Coming to the world, which is also the world's Last Judgment. A German writer put it consolingly:

> Salvation and damnation are equally grounded in the ineluctable decision of God. . . . They do not, however, stand alongside each other having the same rank, for God's universal saving will has been revealed in the gospel of Jesus Christ, whereas God's no is a mystery withdrawn from human knowledge.[1]

In thinking of the glorious Parousia, the mind then focuses more naturally on the salvific consequences of the return of the Lord, rather than the negative implications that attach to this event by virtue of the "General Judgment" of the human race, though both are included in the Parousia mystery to come.

"To come"—yet the very word *parousia* lends itself to the notion, prominent in the New Testament letters, that the reality in question is not entirely future. In some way it is also present, and even, indeed, immediately present.

> Though . . . the primary reference is eschatological, to a definite coming that has not yet been fully manifested, it is impossible not to notice how appropriate the word was to emphasize the nearness and the certainty of that "coming." So near was it that it was not so much a "coming" as already a "presence" of the Lord with his people, a *permanent* presence, moreover, which not even absence from sight for a little while could really interrupt, and which, when fully established, would last for ever.[2]

Michael Ramsey points out how in this regard "parousia" resembles such cognate manifestation words as *epiphaneia* or sudden appearance, *apokalypsis* or disclosure, and *phanerousthai* or manifestation. And he finds that all four words can serve *both* for a "future consummation" *and* for the "original events of the Gospel."[3]

Epiphany, Apocalypse, Manifestation—the appearing of the divine light, the
disclosure of the divine secret, the coming before men's eyes of Christ—these
are things which the Christians await with the conviction that what the future
will bring is but the consummation of a past event and a present possession. [4]

The Transfiguration is, via the Resurrection, the real anticipation of the Parousia in the Christ-narrative: "[T]hough the glory would be His from the
third day, it would become visible to the Church only at His return," a claim
especially emphasized in the Gospel according to Mark. [5] In Second Peter,
meanwhile, the Transfiguration does not only confirm the true of the entire
prophetic teaching that spoke of a messianic age, it also proves the reality of
the coming Parousia of Christ.

Balthasar, in *Theo-drama*, found an inauguration of the Son of man's
reign in the public ministry, and a consummation of that reign only in a
Second Coming. Here he was in agreement with Lagrange:

> That inauguration is discreet, manifested to the apostles to whom is henceforth
> confided its preaching, the recruitment of its subjects, the administration of the
> kingdom (18:18) under the leading of Peter (16:18). The manifestation of the
> second coming, with the angels, will be more solemn, and this is what Mat-
> thew calls *parousia* (24:3, 27, 37, 39), comparing it thus to solemn visits of a
> sovereign to one of his estates. [6]

In his mysteries, from his Birth to his Death and Resurrection, "Jesus fulfils
the Old Testament future expectation, but, arising out of his own person and
the arrival of the kingdom in this world, issue further promises." [7] George
Eldon Ladd, whose presentation Balthasar is summarizing here, had this to
say. "The Kingdom of God involves two great moments: fulfillment within
history, and consummation at the end of history. It is precisely this background which provides the setting for the parables of the Kingdom." [8] "Realized" eschatology—the inaugurated Kingdom—is not meant to be directed
against "futurist" eschatology—the consummated Kingdom to come—but to
draw it into the "central" eschatology that, in Balthasar's view, flows from
Christology itself. [9]

> [A]part from unimportant and incidental vestiges of Jewish eschatology, the
> New Testament no longer entertains the idea of a self-unfolding horizontal
> theo-drama; there is only a vertical theo-drama in which every moment of
> time, insofar as it has Christological significance, is directly related to the
> exalted Lord, who has taken the entire content of all history—life, death and
> resurrection—with him into the supra-temporal realm. [10]

How do the Fathers see it? The theological roots of the image of Christ in
Majesty (the *Majestas* image) would appear to lie in the Nicene dogma. [11]
Athanasius' *homoousion* doctrine licensed the transfer of the title *Pantokra-*

tor from the eternal Father to the co-eternal Son. On this view, the employ-
ment of court motifs from the Roman art of the imperial age is simply the
exploitation of a repertoire of iconographic models that lay conveniently to
hand for the articulation of this theme. That is the judgment of Geir Hellemo,
a Norwegian student of the early Christian eschatology found in the dual
medium of mosaic and catechesis. "When imperially slanted iconography is
utilized in a liturgical context it does not necessarily imply that Christian
imagery has been completely governed by imperial interests and needs. On
the contrary, we find it reasonable that church leaders wished to indicate
particular liturgical points within a process of iconographical development
taking place largely within the church itself. [12] " The patristic Church was not
at the mercy of the Constantinian State.

For Hellemo, the image of Christ as king in palaeo-Christian art may have
regard to his already inaugurated regal office, stemming from the Resurrection and Ascension events. A "futuristic-eschatological" aspect—which the
Parousia mystery requires—cannot be presumed without specific indications.
And yet often enough such indications exist. Thus in a terracotta plaque from
the Barberini Collection, now at the Dumbarton Oaks Center for Byzantine
Studies outside Washington, this aspect

> is so fully developed that it dominates the entire presentation. The plaque is
> divided into two scenes. In the upper section the enthroned Christ is shown
> with six of his apostles. A whip and *tesserae* (entrance tickets) lie by his feet.
> Before him is a latticed balustrade separating him and the apostles from the
> small figures entering from gates on either side. . . . These come to a halt
> before Christ, acclaiming him with lifted hands. This scene is quite rightly
> found to be a depiction of the last judgment. The whip signifies the punish-
> ment of the wicked whereas the *tesserae* represent the reward to the righteous.
> No sinners are shown on the plaque as obviously all the figures in the lower
> zone are facing Christ whom they are hailing. Thus, the act of judgment
> becomes an act of acclamation. [13]

This eloquent artifact suggests how the proportions of New Testament teaching on the mysteries of Christ remained intact. For biblical eschatology, it is
salvation which has the priority, while the possibility of damnation, though
affirmed, is also relegated to a degree of obscurity.

Though the task of the royal judge is focused on human beings, he remains the *Pantokrator*, and thus Lord of the cosmos. In an artwork in a very
different medium, the apse mosaic at Santa Pudenziana in Rome has the
"four living creatures" of Ezekiel's vision, recurring as they do in the Johannine Apocalypse, flank the enthroned Christ and give a cosmic dimension to
his sovereign judicial power.

The Passion and Death of the Lord, his *katabasis*, was the foundation of
his Resurrection and Ascension, the *anabasis*. So the Savior's reference to

the "sign of the Son of Man" in his Apocalyptic Discourse at Matthew 24:30 was widely represented as a reference to the appearance of a cosmic Cross as the prelude to his Parousia—perhaps as early as the *Didache* (and thus before the end of the first century of the Common Era).[14] At Sant'Apollinare at Ravenna a shining cross in the apse "not only refers to Christ's death and resurrection but also to his presence here and now and to his coming on the Last Day."[15] In the *Catecheses* of St. Cyril of Jerusalem, the bishop tells the initiates that the Cross will be the sign of the Lord's coming at the Parousia just as it was at his first advent. In Catechesis 13, the reason why the "trophy of the King" will go before him is that "the Jews, who were responsible for the execution, will recognize him by the cross and pour out their troubles," while "the faithful will be able to acclaim him at that same cross." It is through the Cross that Cyril can relate the "events taking place at the end of time" to the Lord's earthly life as to the lives of Christians.[16] Catechesis 15 describes those events on the basis of the biblical testimony, and they amount to the unconcealed revelation of the Son's divinity in a manner that entails the renewal of the created world, an *anakainopoeisis* or "making new again." Even now, the Cross, when considered as the sign of the Parousia, sends the message that the "consequences of Christ's saving work will only appear at the end of time."[17] In the almost contemporary catechetical instruction of Theodore of Mopsuestia, it is in this liturgical life that "man is put into contact with the new creative act which God applies in this world but which is only made complete at the end of time,"[18] for, in Theodore's words in his catechetical homilies, "We are ordered to perform in this world the symbols and signs of the future things."[19] Here the Eucharistic Anaphora is key since in its course the faithful behold the Sacrifice of Christ—the true reality of the Cross—taking place at the hands of its minister, the icon of the High Priest.[20]

The Cross, then, signs the entire Christian life, its past, present ,and future. Before the Parousia comes, one might say, a continuing Holy Saturday—bearing in mind how, before the reform of the Roman-rite Holy Week in 1955, that day was not only the memorial of the Descent into Hell but also the occasion for the celebration of the Easter Vigil, and therefore pointed ahead to the mysteries of the Resurrection, Ascension, and Pentecost. It was in this manner that Ildefonso Schuster related Holy Saturday to the Parousia of the Lord.

> Faith indeed sustains us, and Hope assures us that one day all the miseries of our mortal nature will cease; but in the meantime we must be content to spend our mystical Holy Saturday in watching and waiting. . . .The true and perfect Easter will indeed come, and when it comes it will exceed all our conceptions. And when shall this be? When Christ shall cease to offer daily by the hands of his priests the Eucharistic mysteries which commemorate his death and shall establish in heaven a new liturgy, the Liturgy of the universal and unending Easter.[21]

St. Thomas treats the Parousia above all in its character of judgment. "Because Christ in his humanity by which he suffered and rose again, promised us both resurrection and eternal life that common judgment whereby those who are rising again are either rewarded or punished belongs fittingly to him: '[The Father] has given him authority to execute judgment, because he is the Son of man' (John 5:27)."[22] This coheres with the closing Resurrection appearance in St. Matthew's Gospel, which is also the scene-setting for an Ascension that remained, in that Gospel book, alluded to but not described. "All authority in heaven and on earth has been given to me" (Matthew 28:18): in his *Commentary on the Gospel of John*, Thomas aligns this text with the saying from the Sabbath discourse of Jesus at Bethzatha just cited.[23] Insofar as the judgment is of visible, embodied human beings, it will, so he stresses, be appropriately visible in form. Christ will judge "in the form of humanity" (*Summa contra Gentiles*), "in human form" (*Commentary on the Gospel of John*), in such a way that all human beings will be able to see him, whatever their moral or salvational status.[24] But the vision of his divinity that will render the redeemed *beati*—this will only be apparent to the good, for the message of the Beatitude is plain: "Blessed are the pure of heart, for they shall see God" (Matthew 5:8).[25] For Thomas, the Judgment at the Parousia will suitably be a mystery of the *incarnate* Word, the Word who has undergone *enanthropesis* to be a man like us, because it was through the "humiliation of the Passion"; that he "promised the glory of exaltation"—and also because such a judgment "insinuates clemency."[26] The humanized Lord is the One chosen to be our Judge, and his closeness to us, as our kin, speaks volumes about the mercy of God.

Balthasar, in speaking of Jesus the Judge of the Glorious Parousia, takes up in his own way this last cue from St. Thomas:

> His identity as a figure of glory cannot be divided from the wounds he received in his work of reconciling, wounds he still manifests as the Risen One. That is why John twice insists he is drawing on the Old Testament source ("they will look on him whom they have pierced" [Zechariah 12:10, cited in John 19:37 and Revelation 1:7] that now reaches its full depth of meaning, and which (in Revelation 1:7) he does not hesitate to combine with the passage from Daniel: "Behold, he is coming on the clouds. Every eye will see him, even those who have pierced him and there will be lamenting over him among all the peoples of the earth. So shall it be! Amen.[27]

The Judge is a figure of power, certainly, yet it is because he has "experienced all forms of sin and abandonment in his own body" that "gives him his highest competence as Judge."[28] So those who "are to be judged by him can draw hope for grace from his powerlessness, his solidarity with sinners and the lost," though (warns Balthasar) they cannot "deduce the outcome of that judgment beforehand."[29]

Bulgakov would insist on the relation between Christ's glory in the Parousia and the hypostasis—the person—of the Holy Spirit, even to the point of speaking of the Second Coming as the Parousia of the Spirit as well. The Christ who sends down the Spirit at Pentecost sends him again at the Parousia, this time as transparent "glory."[30]

And what of post-patristic iconography? The icon of the Second Coming in the Byzantine-Slav tradition remains—as (where it existed) in the ancient Church—the image of Christ enthroned. Andrew Tregubov describes the icon on this theme as painted at Noisy-le-Grand, in France, by the exiled Russian iconographer Gregory Kroug. "The Lord is sitting on His throne surrounded by seraphim. At the four corners of the icon are symbols of the evangelists: an angel, a lion, a bull, and an eagle. The red octagonal star and mandorla behind Christ form an opening into the new reality of the Kingdom of God, the New Jerusalem.[31] As Tregubov explains, "The space of the Kingdom of God is Christocentric, everything measured by Him and pointing to Him."[32] In any icon, "light is the ultimate visual symbol of the glory of God, the sign of His presence," but in this particular icon of "the 'Christ of the Second and Glorious Coming,' truly it can be said that 'as the lightning flashes and lights up the sky from one side to the other, so will the Son of Man be in this day' (Luke 17:24)."[33] The cherubim often attend this enthroned Christ, and, in the West, so do the saints. In St. Matthew's Gospel the Son of Man will come "in the glory of the Father, surrounded by his holy angels" (Matthew 16:27; compare Matthew 25:31), while the co-judges include the Twelve (Matthew 19:28), the representatives of the Church in her holiness. "The Lord promises that at his return he will come in the clouds of heaven, surrounded by the angels and the saints of God. This is how he now appears in prayer."[34] The time of the Church and the time of the End of the Ages intersect. "The cry of longing with which the book of Revelation closes is addressed to a present which is still lingering, not to a future which has not yet come about."[35] The Parousia cannot be participated in the way that other mysteries can, but it can certainly be anticipated. This is the point of Christian hope.

NOTES

1. Udo Schnelle, *Theology of the New Testament* (Grand Rapids, MI: Baker Academic, 2009), 214.

2. George Milligan, *Saint Paul's Epistles to the Thessalonians* (London: MacMillan, 1908), 147, cited in Arthur Michael Ramsey, *The Glory of God and the Transfiguration of Christ* (London: Darton, Longman and Todd, 1967 [1949]), 34.

3. Ramsey, *The Glory of God*, 34.

4. Ramsey, *The Glory of God*, 34–35.

5. Ramsey, *The Glory of God*, 118–19.

6. Marie-Joseph Lagrange, *Evangile selon saint Matthieu* (Paris: Gabalda, 1948, 8th edition), CLXVI.

7. Hans Urs von Balthasar, *Theo-Drama. Theological Dramatic Theory, V: The Last Act*, (San Francisco, CA: Ignatius, 1998), 27.

8. George Eldon Ladd, *Jesus and the Kingdom: The Eschatology of Biblical Realism* (London: SPCK, 1966), 214. This work was subsequently reissued under the title *The Presence of the Future* (London: SPCK, 1974).

9. Hans Urs von Balthasar, *Theo-Drama*, 26.

10. Hans Urs von Balthasar, *Theo-Drama*, 48.

11. Per Beskow, *The Kingship of Christ in the Early Church* (Stockholm: Almquist & Wiksell, 1952).

12. Geir Hellemo, *Adventus Domini: Eschatological Thought in Fourth Century Apses and Catecheses* (Leiden and New York: Brill, 1989), 14.

13. Hellemo, *Adventus Domini*, 50.

14. *Didache* 16:6.

15. Hellemo, *Adventus Domini*, 113.

16. Hellemo, *Adventus Domini*, 179.

17. Hellemo, *Adventus Domini*, 179.

18. Hellemo, *Adventus Domini*, 246–47.

19. Alphonse Mingana (ed.), *Commentary of Theodore of Mopsuestia on the Lord's Prayer and on the Sacraments of Baptism and the Eucharist* (Cambridge: Cambridge University Press, 1933), 82, quoted by Geir Hellemo, *Adventus Domini*, 231.

20. Ibid., 231–32.

21. Ildefonso Schuster, *The Sacramentary (Liber Sacramentorum): Historical and Liturgical Notes on the Roman Missal* (London: Burns, Oates and Washbourne, 1924), II., 227.

22. Thomas Aquinas, *Summa contra Gentiles* IV, 96.

23. Aquinas, *Commentary on the Gospel of St. John* 2, lect. 2.

24. Aquinas, *Summa contra Gentiles* IV, 96; *Commentary on the Gospel of St. John* 2, lect. 2.

25. Cited ibid.

26. Ibid.

27. Hans Urs von Balthasar, "Eschatology in Outline," in *Explorations in Theology IV: Spirit and Institution* (San Francisco: Ignatius, 1995), 423–68, and here at 447–48.

28. Hans Urs von Balthasar, *Explorations in Theology* IV, 449.

29. Hans Urs von Balthasar, *Explorations in Theology* IV, 449.

30. Sergius Bulgakov, *The Bride of the Lamb* (Grand Rapids, MI: Eerdmans, 2002), 398.

31. Andrew Tregubov, *The Light of Christ: Iconography of Gregory Kroug* (Crestwood, NY: St. Vladimir's Seminary Press, 1990), 10.

32. Tregubov, *The Light of Christ*, 10.

33. Tregubov, *The Light of Christ*, 10.

34. Hans Urs von Balthasar, *Prayer* (San Francisco, CA: Ignatius, 1986), 85.

35. Hans Urs von Balthasar, *Prayer*, 282.

Conclusion

Balthasar wrote, "As we observe how the incarnate Son relates to the Father, we see the archetype within the godhead, and, within it, we see what the creature is meant to be according to the Father's eternal vision of it; of itself, of its own creaturely nature, it cannot fulfil this vision: to do this, the Son must elevate the creature into his own relationship with the Father, a relationship which is divine, and to that extent inaccessible to the creature."[1] In a nutshell, that is why all human beings need to know the "Deep Mysteries," that bind into one God, Christ and ourselves. But to know them at the level of their own being requires the activity of the Holy Spirit. "Through the Spirit we can look at the Son; sharing in his Spirit we are permitted to understand him. And through the Son we are led into the Spirit of the Father, who is one Spirit with that of the Son.[2] Thus Balthasar, and we may add Bulgakov's last words in "Oration on the day of Pentecost."

> And now this divine descent is revealed fully: The Lord not only created the world but also came to dwell in it—the Father by the Son and by the Holy Spirit.[3]

Reading a book like the present one can give us a surmise of the Mystery of the triune God disclosed in the mysteries of Christ. But only the Spirit, as divine Mystagogue, can initiate us into the depths. There, in and through the events of the life, Death, and Exaltation of Christ—and the term "exaltation" here will include the Christ of Pentecost and the Parousia—we can have access to the eternal self-surrendering, self-sacrificial love that the Holy Trinity is.

NOTES

1. Hans Urs von Balthasar, *Prayer* (San Francisco, CA: Ignatius, 1986), 186.
2. Hans Urs von Balthasar, *Prayer*, 192.
3. Sergius Bulgakov, *Churchly Joy: Orthodox Devotions for the Church* Year (Grand Rapids, MI: Eerdmans, 2008), 131.

Bibliography

Armitage, J. Mark. *A Twofold Solidarity: Leo the Great's Theology of Redemption*. Strathfield, NSW: St Paul's Publications, 2005.

Bataillon, Louis-Jacques, O. P. "Saint Thomas et les Pères: De la Catena à la Tertia Pars," in *Ordo sapientiae et amoris. Image et message de saint Thomas d'Aquin à travers les récentes études historiques, herméneutiques et doctrinales. Hommage au professeur Jean-Pierre Torrell à l'occasion de son 65e anniversaire*, edited by Carlos-Josaphat Pinto da Oliveira, 1–6. Fribourg: Editions universitaires, 1993.

Bauckham, Richard. *God Crucified: Monotheism and Christology in the New Testament*. Carlisle: Paternoster, 1998.

———. *Jesus and the Eyewitnesses: The Gospels as Eyewitness Testimony*. Grand Rapids, MI: Eerdmans, 2006.

Belting, Hans. *Likeness and Presence: A History of the Image before the Era of Art*. Chicago, IL, and London: University of Chicago Press, 1994.

Beskow, Per. *The Kingship of Christ in the Early Church*. Stockholm: Almquist and Wiksell, 1952.

Bieler, Martin. "God and the Cross: The Doctrine of God in the Work of Hans Urs von Balthasar." *Communio* 42 (2015): 61–88.

Blomberg, Craig L. *The Historical Reliability of the Gospels*. Leicester: Inter-Varsity Press, 1987.

———. *The Historical Reliability of John's Gospel: Issues and Commentary*. Downers Grove, IL: IVP Academic Press, 2002.

Brown, Raymond E. *The Gospel according to John [i–xii]*. London, Chapman, 1971.

———. *The Birth of the Messiah: A Commentary on the Infancy Narratives in Matthew and Luke*. New York, NY: Image Books, 1979 [1977].

Bulgakov, Sergius. *The Bride of the Lamb* Grand Rapids, MI: Eerdmans, 2002.

———. *Churchly Joy: Orthodox Devotions for the Church Year*. Grand Rapids, MI: Eerdmans, 2008.

Bunge, Gabriel. *Rublev's Trinity*. Crestwood, NY: St Vladimir's Seminary Press, 2007.

Chifflot, Thomas G., O. P. "Le Christ et le temps," *La Maison-Dieu* 13 (1948): 26–49.

Childs, Brevard. "Prophecy and Fulfilment: A Study of Contemporary Hermeneutics." *Interpretation* 12 (1958): 259–71.

Chilton, Bruce, and Craig A. Evans, ed. *Authenticating the Activities of Jesus*. Leiden: Brill, 1999.

Corbin, Michel. "La Parole devenue chair: Lecture de la première question de la *Tertia Pars* de la *Somme théologique* de Thomas d'Aquin." *Revue des sciences philosophiques et théologiques* 67 (1978): 5–40.

Dalmais, Irénée-Henri, O. P. "Le dimanche dans la Liturgie byzantine." *La Maison-Dieu* 46 (1956): 60–66.

Dalmais, Irénée-Henri, Pierre Jounel, and Aimé Georges Martimort. *The Church at Prayer, An Introduction to the Liturgy, IV: The Liturgy and Time*. London: Chapman, 1986.

Dalman, Gustaf. *Jesus-Jeshua: Studies in the Gospels*. New York, NY: Macmillan, 1929.

———. *Sacred Sites and Ways: Studies in the Topography of the Gospels*. London: SPCK, 1935.

de Grandmaison, Léonce, S. J. *Jésus Christ, Sa personne, son message, ses oeuvres*. 2nd ed. Vols. 1–2. Paris: Beauchesne, 1928.

de la Taille, Maurice, S. J. *Mysterium fidei: De augustissimo corporis et sanguinis Christi sacrificio et sacramento*. Vols. 1–2. Paris: Beauchesne, 1921.

de Soos, Marie Bernard. *Le mystère liturgique d'après saint Léon le Grand*. Münster: Aschendorff, 1958.

Drobner, Hubertus R. *The Fathers of the Church: A Comprehensive Introduction*. Peabody, MA: Hendrickson, 2007.

Dungan, David L. *The Sayings of Jesus in the Churches of Paul*. Philadelphia, PN: Fortress, 1971.

Emery, Gilles. O. P., *La Trinité créatrice: Trinité et Création dans les commentaries aux Sentences de Thomas d'Aquin et de ses précurseurs Albert le Grand et Bonaventure*. Paris: Vrin, 1994.

———. "Trinité et creation: Le principe trinitaire de la création dans les Commentaires d'Albert le Grand, de Bonaventure et de Thomas d'Aquin sur less Sentences." *Revue des sciences philosophiques et théologiques* 79 (1995): 405–30.

Farrer, Austin. "An English Appreciation," in *Kerygma and Myth: A Theological Debate*, edited by Hans Werner Bartsch, 212–23. London: SPCK, 1953.

Galot, Jean. S. J., *Dieu, souffre-t-il?* Paris: Lethellieux, 1976.

Gamble, Harry Y. *Books and Readers in the Early Church: A History of Early Christian Texts*. New Haven, CT: Yale University Press, 1995.

Gerhardsson, Birger. *The Reliability of the Gospel Tradition*. Peabody, MA: Hendrickson, 2001.

Grierson. Roderick. ed. *Gates of Mystery: The Art of Holy Russia*. Fort Worth, TX: InterCultura, 2007.

Hart, David Bentley. "A Gift Exceeding Every Debt: An Eastern Orthodox Appreciation of Anselm's *"Cur Deus homo."* *Pro Ecclesia* VII, no. 3 (1998): 333–49.

Hellemo, Geir. *Adventus Domini: Eschatological Thought in Fourth Century Apses and Catecheses*. Leiden and New York, NY: Brill, 1989.

Hengel, Martin. "Jesus, the Messiah of Israel: The Debate about the 'Messianic Mission' of Jesus," in *Authenticating the Activities of Jesus*, edited by Bruce Chilton and Craig A. Evans, 323–49. Leiden: Brill, 1999.

———. *The Septuagint as Christian Scripture*. Edinburgh: T. and T. Clark, 2002.

Hill, Charles E. *The Johannine Corpus in the Early Church*. Oxford: Oxford University Press, 2004.

Hodgson, Leonard. *The Doctrine of the Atonement*. New York, NY: Charles Scribner and Sons, 1951.

Hurtado, Larry W. *Lord Jesus Christ: Devotion to Jesus in Earliest Christianity*. Grand Rapids, MH, and Cambridge: Eerdmans, 2005.

———. *One God, One Lord: Early Christian Devotion and Ancient Jewish Monotheism*. 3rd. ed. London: Bloomsbury T and T Clark, 2015.

Jaschke, Hans-Jochen. *Der Heilige Geist im Bekenntnis der Kirche: Eine Studie zur Pneumatologie des Irenäus von Lyon im Ausgang vom altchristlichen Glaubensbekenntnis*. Münster: Aschendorff, 1976.

Kartsonis, Anna. *Anastasis, the Making of an Image*. Princeton, NJ: Princeton University Press, 1986.

Koen, Lars. *The Saving Passion: Incarnational and Soteriological Thought in Cyril of Alexandria's Commentary on the Gospel according to St John*. Stockholm: Almqvist and Wiksell, 1991.

Ladd, George Eldon. *Jesus and the Kingdom: The Eschatology of Biblical Realism.* London: SPCK, 1966.

Lagrange, Marie-Joseph. O. P., *The Gospel of Jesus Christ.* London: Burns, Oates and Washbourne, 1938.

———. *Evangile selon saint Marc.* Paris: Gabalda, 1947.

———. *Evangile selon saint Matthieu.* 8th ed. Paris: Gabalda, 1948.

Lossky, Vladimir, and Leonid Ouspensky. *The Meaning of Icons.* Crestwood, NY: St Vladimir's Seminary Press, 1982.

Marmion, Columba. *Christ in His Mysteries.* Bethesda, MD: Zacchaeus Press, 2008.

Martin, Jennifer Newsome. *Hans Urs von Balthasar and the Critical Appropriation of Russian Religious Thought.* Notre Dame, IN: University of Notre Dame Press, 2015.

Mother Mary and Archimandrite Kallistos Ware, trans. *The Festal Menaion.* London: Faber and Faber, 1969.

———. *The Lenten Triodion.* London: Faber and Faber, 1978.

Matthiesen, Michon M. *Sacrifice as Gift: Eucharist, Grace and Contemplative Prayer in Maurice de la Taille.* Washington, DC: Catholic University of America Press, 2013.

Mingana. Alphonse, ed. *Commentary of Theodore of Mopsuestia on the Lord's Prayer and on the Sacraments of Baptism and the Eucharist.* Cambridge: Cambridge University Press, 1933.

Müller, Mogens. *The First Bible of the Church: A Plea for the Septuagint.* Sheffield: Sheffield Academic Press, 1996.

McArthur, Allan. *The Evolution of the Christian Year.* London: SCM Press, 1953.

McGuckin, John Anthony. *The Transfiguration of Christ in Scripture and Tradition.* Lewiston, NY: Edwin Mellen Press, 1987.

Narcisse, Gilbert. *Les raisons de Dieu: Argument de convenance et esthétique théologique selon saint Thomas d'Aquin et Hans Urs von Balthasar.* Fribourg: Editions universitaires, 1997.

Nichols, Aidan. O. P., *Chalice of God. A Systematic Theology in Outline.* Collegeville, MN, Liturgical Press, 2012.

O'Hanlon, Gerard, S. J. *The Immutability of God in the Theology of Hans Urs von Balthasar.* Cambridge: Cambridge University Press, 1990.

Pannenberg, Wolfhart. *An Introduction to Systematic Theology.* Grand Rapids, MI: Eerdmans, 1991.

Pixner, Bargil. O. S. B., *With Jesus through Galilee according to the Fifth Gospel.* Rosh Pina: Corazin Publishing, 1992.

Ramsey, Arthur Michael, *The Glory of God and the Transfiguration of Christ.* London: Darton, Longman and Todd, 1967 [1949].

———. *Sacred and Secular.* London: Longmans, 1965.

Ratzinger, Joseph. "Die Bedeutung der Väter im Aufbau des Glaubens," in *Theologische Prinzipienlehre: Bausteine zur Fundamentaltheologie,* edited by Joseph Ratzinger, 139–58. Munich: Erich Wewel, 1982.

Robinson, John A. T. *Redating the New Testament.* London: SCM Press, 1976.

———. *The Priority of John.* London: SCM, 1985.

Saward, John. *The Mysteries of March: Hans Urs von Balthasar on the Incarnation and Easter.* London: Collins, 1990.

Schenk, Richard. O. P. *"Omnis Christi actio fuit nostra instruction:* The Deeds and Sayings of Jesus as Revelation in the View of Thomas Aquinas," in *La doctrine de la Révélation divine,* edited by Leo Elders, S. V. D., 103–31. Vatican City: Vatican Polyglot press, 1990.

Schiller, Gertrud. *Iconography of Christian Art (Vol. 2): The Passion of Jesus Christ.* London: Lund Humphries, 1972.

Schmemann, Alexander. *The Eucharist, Sacrament of the Kingdom.* Crestwood, NY: St Vladimir's Seminary Press, 1987.

Schnelle, Udo. *Theology of the New Testament.* Grand Rapids, MI: Baker Academic, 2009.

Schuster, Ildefonso. *The Sacramentary (Liber Sacramentorum): Historical and Liturgical Notes on the Roman Missal.* Vols. 1–5. London: Burns, Oates and Washbourne, 1924.

Shalina, Irina. "The Descent into Hell (Anastasis) with Saints," in *Gates of Mystery: The Art of Holy Russia*, edited by Roderick Grierson, 219–25. Fort Worth: Intercultura, 2007).

Sottocornola, Franco. *L'Anno liturgico nei sermoni di Pietro Crisologo*. Cesena: Centro studi e ricerche sulla antica provincia ecclesiastica ravennate, 1973.

Stanton, Graham. *Gospel Truth? Today's Quest for Jesus of Nazareth*. 2nd. ed. London: Collins, 1997.

Stewart-Sykes, Alistair. *The Lamb's High Feast: Melito, Peri Pacha, and the Quartodeciman Paschal Liturgy at Sardis*. Leiden: Brill, 1998.

Taylor, Vincent. *The Formation of the Gospel Tradition*. 2nd ed. London: Macmillan, 1933.

Torrell, Jean-Pierre. *Le Christ en ses Mystères: La vie et l'oeuvre de Jésus selon saint Thomas d'Aquin*. Vols. 1–2. Paris: Desclée, 1999.

Tregubov, Andrew. *The Light of Christ: Iconography of Gregory Kroug*. Crestwood, NY: St Vladimir's Seminary Press, 1990.

Vetö, Etienne. *Du Christ à la Trinité: Penser les Mystères du Christ après Thomas d'Aquin et Balthasar*. Paris, Editions du Cerf, 2012.

von Balthasar, Hans Urs. *The God-question and Modern Man*. New York, NY: Seabury, 1967.

———. *The Glory of the Lord. A Theological Aesthetics, I. Seeing the Form*. Edinburgh: T. and T. Clark, 1982.

———. *The Threefold Garland*. San Francisco, CA: Ignatius, 1982.

———. *You Crown the Year with your Goodness*. San Francisco, CA: Ignatius, 1982.

———. *Prayer*. San Francisco, CA: Ignatius, 1986.

———. *Explorations in Theology I: The Word Made Flesh*. San Francisco, CA: Ignatius, 1989.

———. *The Glory of the Lord: A Theological Aesthetics, VII: The New Covenant*. Edinburgh: T. and T. Clark, 1989.

———. *Mysterium Paschale: The Mystery of Easter*. Edinburgh: T. and T. Clark, 1990.

———. *Explorations in Theology IV: Spirit and Institution*. San Francisco, CA: Ignatius, 1995.

———. *Theo-Drama: Theological Dramatic Theory, V: The Last Act*. San Francisco, CA: Ignatius, 1998.

Ward, Sister Benedicta. S. L. G., trans. *The Prayers and Meditations of St Anselm*. London: Penguin, 1973.

Weitzmann, Kurt. *The Monastery of Saint Catherine at Mount Sinai: The Icons. Volume I: From the Sixth to the Tenth Century*. Princeton, NJ: Princeton University Press, 1976.

Wenham, David. *Paul: Follower of Jesus or Founder of Christianity?* Grand Rapids, MI: Eerdmans, 1995.

Wenham, John. *Easter Enigma*. Exeter: Paternoster Press, 1984.

———. *Redating Matthew, Mark and Luke: A Fresh Assault on the Synoptic Problem*. London: Hodder and Stoughton, 1991.

Winslow, Donald F. *The Dynamics of Salvation : A Study in Gregory of Nazianzus*. Cambridge, MA: Philadelphia Patristic Foundation, 1979.

Wright, N. T. *Who Was Jesus?* London: SPCK, 1992.

Index

About the Author

Aidan Nichols, born 1948, is a Dominican friar who has taught theology in Italy, England, the United States, Ethiopia, and the West Indies. He held the John Paul II Memorial Lectureship in Roman Catholic Theology and was for many years a Member of the Cambridge University Faculty of Divinity. He has published over fifty books on a variety of topics in fundamental, historical, ecumenical theology as well as on the relation of religion to literature and art.